O9-BTZ-435

The Beer Can

by Beer Can Collectors of America
Edited by Larry Wright #2

Greatlakes Living Press, Publishers
3634 W. 216th St.
Matteson, Illinois 60443

THE BEER CAN
© Beer Can Collectors of America 1976
International Standard Book Number: 0-915498-25-1
Library of Congress Catalog Card Number: 76-3354
All rights reserved
Printed in U.S.A.

Special Editing:
    Charles A. Nekvasil #525, Cleveland, Ohio
    Tom Teague #1242, Springfield, Illinois

Research:
    Jack Sheahan #225, Washington, D.C.

Some photos by:
    Lew Cady #98, Denver, Colorado
    Gene Milkowski #465, Dolton, Illinois

Original cover design by:
    Richard Schlater #519, Battle Creek, Michigan

Cover photos by:
    Jack Martells #3532, Palos Heights, Illinois

CONTENTS

ACKNOWLEDGEMENTS

The hobby of beer can collecting, since 1970, has grown from perhaps a few hundred to a few hundred thousand — and is still growing by leaps and bounds. It is surely today's fastest growing collecting hobby.

Several beer can catalog-type books and booklets have been offered during the past two years by Beer Can Collectors of America and others. However, this is the first book to cover the entire spectrum of the hobby, from the history of the can to swapping and restoring.

Beer Can Collectors of America wishes to thank the following BCCA members for their research and writing talents in making this book possible.

[*Note: Numbers following names are BCCA membership numbers.*]

Chapter One
John R. Krueger #107, Bloomington, Indiana
Don Kurtz #891, Portage, Indiana

Chapter Two
Richard J. LaSusa #609, Carol Stream, Illinois
Robert Myers #26, Oakland, California

Chapter Three
Robert Eckert #3, Des Peres, Missouri
Larry Wright #2, St. Louis, Missouri

Chapter Four
Denver Wright, Jr. #1, St. Louis, Missouri
Louise Durbin #859, Hamilton, Ohio

Chapter Five
Bill Christensen #33, Madison, New Jersey
John Zembo #567, Austin, Texas
Clyde L. Hooker #2985, Bemidji, Minnesota

Chapter Six
Gil Brennell #13, St. Louis, Missouri
C. D. Roberts #278, Cottage Grove, Minnesota
Tom Williams #114, Springfield, Illinois
Bob Corbett #3235, Webster Groves, Missouri
Tom Wiegand #1910, Long Island, New York
Bill Christensen #33, Madison, New Jersey

This book is dedicated to our friend, the Beer Can.

For information about other Beer Can Collectors of America publications and membership, write to:

Beer Can Collectors of America
7500 Devonshire
St. Louis, Missouri 63119

Jumping On
The "Canned" Wagon

The beer can, emblematic of today's throwaway culture, has been with us just over 40 short, though tumultuous years, but it has a family tree with roots stretching back almost 8,000 years. Brewing itself was one of the first arts known to man, beginning prior to Old Testament times with accidental fermentation of grains and fruits. In fact, there is even evidence of early brewing in Mesopotamia in 6,000 B.C. Some ancient beverages were similar to modern day beer, brewed from malts or grains, while others were meads or wines.

The first recorded appearance of beer in America was in 1584, but this scarcely compares to several European breweries, which proudly trace their heritage back to the Fourteenth century.

Our ancestors experimented with a variety of ways to preserve food and drink. Some of the first containers they used were large pottery jars, animal skins, wooden casks or barrels, gourds, and other hollowed-out vegetable receptacles. The first canning process was perfected in France in the early Nineteenth Century, using specially made glass bottles sealed by heat pressure. Englishman Peter Durand read about the French achievement and carried it one step further, replacing the fragile bottles with cylindrical cannisters fashioned out of tin plate. In 1810, King George III granted him a patent for the world's first can.

In 1825, Thomas Kensett and Ezra Daggett were granted the first American patent for preserving foods in "vessels of tin." The canning industry grew rapidly here, as the new invention proved the cheapest container for mass production. The invention of high speed equipment that could fill cans at the rate of more than 100 a minute spurred its growth. Early cans held fruit, vegetables, meat, and some beverages, and their use had become quite widespread by the Civil War.

Even though canning technology was highly sophisticated long before the turn of this century, it took more than 100 years after the can's introduction to successfully can beer. While canning most foods takes a pressure of only 25 to 30 pounds per square inch, beer requires 80 to 90 pounds. Consequently, a much sturdier container was needed: walls had to be stout enough to resist the triple-fold pressure, but at the same time had to remain sufficiently workable to form the side seam.

The primary reason for the beer can's tardy advent, however, was that beer reacts strongly upon contact with metal, creating salts which give the brew an unpleasant taste. Obviously, if canned beer tasted more like the can than beer, it wouldn't play well in Peoria.

Can Companies' research scientists began experimenting with various types of beer cans in the 1920s, coating their prototypes with a wide variety of linings to keep the beer from coming in contact with the metal. Plastics provided the answer, with American Can's "Vinylite" leading the way. It was later refined into a high temperature baked enamel, made of natural and synthetic resins. Since then, canners have developed many other can coatings, chiefly of the polymeric variety.

But can companies and brewers alike knew that, technology or not, the beer can faced a long uphill battle to gain public acceptance. Aside from taverns where kegs were used, the glass bottle had dominated beer packaging for decades. And beer bottles themselves were only a small part of the glass container industry, which was also filling its product with milk, soda pop, medicine, wine, liquor, and dozens of other liquids. Over the years, a complex machinery had evolved around the bottle. Unlike the can, it not only had to be made and filled, but also gathered up after use, stored, shipped, scrubbed, disinfected, relabeled, and refilled as often as 25 times.

With the bottle so well entrenched, neither glass companies nor brewers were anxious to witness the beer can's birth. Glass companies, of course, wanted to protect their market; brewers had millions invested in bottling equipment. To top it off, the beer can was initially far costlier than the bottle.

Fortunately, the can had some pluses, too. It was shorter, smaller, and lighter than the bottle, so it cost much less to ship. But most of all, it could be thrown right into the trash heap when empty (fortunately for can collectors, this wasn't always what happened).

Still, bottled beer wasn't about to step down from its throne. After decades of drinking beer from those clear, sanitary containers, people were naturally skeptical about drinking from something you couldn't see through, had been God knows where, had uncounted bugs in it, and needed special instructions and implements to be opened.

A strong element of consumer psychology was at work, so bottle proponents quickly seized upon all cases of evidence showing that beer cans were of questionable quality or even outright dangerous. Stories circulated about people who had become ill or even died after drinking beer from cans. Bringing science to their aid, bottle companies tried to show can linings were unsafe and would deteriorate with age, that metal poisoning cases were being kept out of newspapers, that all kinds of vermin hid in the opaque cans, and so forth. The anti-can prejudice persisted in spite of one famous incident when a brewmaster scraped the linings from three cans and consumed them with no ill effects.

So, it was with mixed feelings that on January 24, 1935, the American Can Company and Gottfried Krueger Brewing Company of New Jersey marketed the world's first beer can—Krueger Cream Ale. Bearing the "Keglined" vinylite trademark, the can was a "flat top" (today's universal shape).

American Can had been dickering with Krueger for a long time about test marketing a can. Krueger had insisted on a careful study of marketing areas first. It wanted a special type of city: neither too large nor too small, and its sales and distribution patterns had to be such that the newcomer's impact could be clearly measured. Richmond, Virginia, seemed to meet those requirements.

No one would admit it at the time, but there was another important reason. Krueger, well established on the Atlantic seaboard, obviously felt it was gambling its good name in this venture and didn't want to risk failure of the new product in its home area. Richmond was far enough away so that if canned beer did turn out to be a colossal failure, sales back home wouldn't be adversely affected. In addition, it was only ale that was being canned, not beer.

Test results weren't long in coming. Within two months, Krueger Cream Ale had upset the market pattern, capturing a large portion of sales from such national brewing giants as Anheuser-Busch, Pabst, and Schlitz. The can's chances for success looked bright.

Large and small breweries alike watched developments closely, and many of the small ones quickly signed up with American Can. But American, realizing it needed more than small regional breweries to make an impact on the total beer market, was anxious to sign up a national power. This came in July, when Pabst began canning its blue and silver Export label (its leading brand, Blue Ribbon, wasn't canned at first). Continental Can Company captured Schlitz in September, 1935. By the end of the year, 23 brewers had jumped on the canned wagon, and the can versus bottle battle was underway.

Economic reasons weighed heavily as cans slowly overtook bottles in sales. Brewers were naturally reluctant to scrap their multi-million dollar investment in bottling equipment, then invest many more millions in canning machinery. The cone top can, however, offered an early solution to this dilemma. Shaped like a container of automotive additive, it could be processed on slightly modified bottling lines.

Whatever the shape, brewers could fill cans faster than bottles.

THE RICHMOND NEWS LEADER, THURSDAY, JANUARY 24, 1935

For your greater convenience and enjoyment

KRUEGER'S *now presents the*

KEGLINED* CAN

(Holds 12 ounces — the same as a bottle)

for ALE *and* BEER

LEFT—*Wood and metal beer kegs are* **COMPLETELY LINED IN-SIDE** *to protect flavor. So is our Keglined Can.*

RIGHT—*Now your Ale and Beer are* **FULLY PROTECTED FROM LIGHT**—*the enemy of flavor. Beer and Ale exposed to light gradually lose flavor.*

LEFT—*Your personal container.* **NO DEPOSIT TO MAKE—NO BOTTLES TO RETURN.** *You simply throw away the empty can.*

RIGHT—*Holds just as much as a bottle—yet* **TAKES ONLY HALF THE SPACE.** *Here's convenience you'll like—in your kitchen—in your ice-box.*

KRUEGER'S CREAM ALE
COOL BEFORE SERVING

Here's the biggest news since repeal—it's the news of a modern way—a more convenient way—to enjoy Krueger's Cream Ale (formerly Boar's Head) in your home. Krueger's, always in the vanguard of brewing science, is the *first* to offer you the advantages of the new keglined can . . . advantages that are truly amazing.

Imagine buying Ale or Beer for your home without paying a bottle deposit, without the trouble and effort of making bottle returns! Imagine being able to get twice as much in the same space in your ice-box! These are the modern conveniences made possible by the astounding keglined can. Of course, you can get your Krueger's in bottles as usual, but we urge you to be one of the first to enjoy the benefits of this remarkable

*REG. U. S. PAT. OFF.

keglined can development. Get a can of Krueger's Cream Ale or Krueger's Finest Beer today! G. Krueger Brewing Company, Newark, N. J.

Richmond Distributor:
CAVALIER DISTRIBUTING CORP.   •   RICHMOND, VA.   •   TEL. 4-8177

Be sure to ask your dealer for a "Quick & Easy" opener and learn the simple little trick of opening your can of ale or beer.

KRUEGER'S CREAM ALE

AND KRUEGER'S *Finest* BEER   *also in bottles and on draught*

This advertisement is not intended to advertise or offer alco holic beverages for sale or delivery in any state, territory, or locality contrary to the laws thereof.

First beer can advertisement.

This meant higher production, increased sales, and additional profits. By the mid-1950s, though, the cone top was nearly extinct. It wasn't as easy to ship or store as the flat top, so brewers switched to the flat top as equipment grew old. Nevertheless, the cone top's shape gives it a special place in the can's history. Many newcomers to the hobby mistakenly believe it was the first type of beer can. However, Schlitz came out with the first Continental Can Company cone in September, 1935.

To counter the can's early success, the glass container industry brought out the stubby bottle. It was shorter and lighter than the regular bottle, so transportation and storage costs were less. Not coincidentally, it was also non-returnable.

Beer can sales increased steadily in the early years, from 200 million in 1935 to more than a billion in 1941. During World War II, however, tin and steel shortages caused a sharp cutback in production. Most canned beer during the war years was marked specifically for consumption by the armed forces, with the brand's design in a black outline against a uniform olive drab background. Now a prize in anybody's collection, this type of container is known as the camouflage can.

After the war, can sales picked up again, as brewers replaced old bottling equipment with canning lines. It still wasn't until 1969, though, that can sales reached the 18 billion mark and replaced the bottle as the most frequently used beer container. Some 35 years after its introduction, the beer can finally came of age.

Suggested Readings

1. "Beer into Cans", in FORTUNE Magazine, January, 1936, pages 74-84.

   A first-class article, written in the first year after introduction of canned beer, giving many facts and figures, and much information about canning and bottling. The source of much information in the present chapter. Highly recommended.

2. Robert Myers, "Some Thoughts . . . On the Beer Can's first 35 Years". 12-page large-size booklet, published by the author, Box 1002, Civic Center Station, Oakland, California 94604.

   Fascinating account of the introduction of the first beer cans, advantages of canned beer, competition between cans and bottles. Also gives valuable tips in estimating can age, including patent numbers and trademark identifications. Highly recommended.

3. Encyclopaedia Britannica, vols. 3 and 4, articles on "BREWING", "BEER", and "CANNING, COMMERICAL".

   Well-written articles giving historical background on these subjects. In place of the Britannica, other encyclopaedias also will have similar articles on these topics, which will be well worth referring to.

by John R. Krueger #107 et al

I never saw
a can
I didn't like!

Can Companies

"Keglined," "Cap-Sealed," "Crowntainer," "National."

Not exactly household words. But in the colorful 40-year history of the beer can, those appellations have been among the most prized possessions of one of America's giant industries—trademarks of the nation's leading can manufacturers.

TRADEMARKS. Words or symbols on a label. The small print tucked away on a quiet side of a beer can; of little importance, other than to their owners, the competitors in the highly competitive worlds of packaging and marketing, and to thousands in the growing legions of beer can collectors.

Those seemingly unobtrusive words have played major roles in the birth and development of the beer can, with little question one of American industry's most successful success stories.

In 40 years, the beer can, the product of the creative genius of the can manufacturing industry, has vaulted from the realm of uncertainty and chance to the dominant position in beer packaging.

The American Can Co. (Keglined), Continental Can Co. (Cap-Sealed), Crown, Cork & Seal Co. (Crowntainer), and National Can Co. (National) are the giants of the can industry in the United States. They, along with a number of smaller manufacturers and a few major brewers, are now producing beer cans at the rate of more than 20 billion annually—about 100 cans for each person in the U.S. They produced more than 24 billion beer cans (tin-free and aluminum) that eventually held more than 70 billion barrels of the brewmaster's golden brew in 1973, exceeding the beer can's closest competitor—the one-way glass bottle—by nearly 18 billion units.

The American brewing industry spent an estimated $1.07 billion for packaging in 1973 (cans plus one-way and returnable bottles), and the can makers garnered the lion's share of that total.

"The impact of the can industry on American brewing has been nothing less than spectacular," said Santo Barea, secretary-treasurer of the Can Manufacturers Institute in Washington, DC. It is a broadly based organization that serves the can manufacturing industry.

Production statistics compiled by the Institute provide a clear picture of the beer can's rise to prominence. (The statistics begin with 1950. Those compiled prior to 1950 are of questionable accuracy. Production totals did not include aluminum cans until 1964.)

Year	Number of beer cans produced (in billions)	Year	Number of beer cans produced (in billions)
1950	5.1	1962	9.0
1951	4.4	1963	9.6
1952	5.1	1964	10.7
1953	6.4	1965	11.3
1954	6.6	1966	12.9
1955	7.4	1967	13.7
1956	7.9	1968	16.0
1957	8.1	1969	18.1
1958	8.4	1970	19.6
1959	9.1	1971	20.0
1960	8.9	1972	21.8
1961	8.7	1973	24.0

The most significant year in this period is 1969, when the total number of beer cans produced exceeded beer bottle production for the first time—52 per cent to 48 per cent (24 per cent each for one-way and returnable bottles).

The can's share of the package beer market is now 60 per cent of the nearly 33 million beer containers produced annually.

The exact breakdown of beer can production by individual company is among the most tightly held secrets in U.S. industry. "Competition for the beer packaging dollar is extremely rugged, so can manufacturers jealously guard their production figures," said a spokesman for one can maker.

However, he was able to provide solid estimates of the various companies' shares of beer can production:

Company	% of Market
American	34
Continental	31
National	12
Reynolds	10a
Crown, Cork & Seal	7
All others	6b
	100

(a: The Reynolds Metals Co. is the largest producer of aluminum beer cans.

(b: These include the Jeffco division of Ball Corp. of Muncie, Indiana, which produces beer cans for the Anheuser-Busch, Inc., brewery at Williamsburg, Virginia, and a few major brewers that are making their own cans.)

One of the most significant developments in recent years is the entry of a handful of major brewers into the can-making field. The Adolph Coors Co. of Golden, Colorado, manufactured all of the 2.46 billion beer cans it used in 1973, and the Jos. Schlitz Co. of Milwaukee, Wisconsin, has plants in operation or under construction to produce millions of beer cans at Milwaukee, Los Angeles, Tampa, Florida, and Longview, Texas.

When the F. & M. Schaefer Brewing Co. dedicated its facility (Conoplant) for making tin-free steel, welded and necked-in cans at its brewery in Albany, New York, Fred W. Hoover, executive vice president—metals operation of Continental Can Co., which participated with Schaefer in the can-making venture, noted that:

"Not very long ago, the conceptual 'seed' of the 'in-plant' manufacture of cans was planted by the two major can companies (American and Continental) to improve their position in the highly competitive world of packaging. . .The(se) fruits or cost savings resulting from the adoption of new concepts have become a most critical factor in our continued growth."

The Schaefer Conoplant was built on the brewery site and the brewery then leased it back to Continental, which retains ownership of the can-making machinery.

According to Rudolph J. Schaefer III, president and board chairman of the Schaefer Brewing Co., ". . .this sophisticated Conoplant process reflects a tremendous amount of . . . ingenuity on the part of Continental and Schaefer engineering and operating personnel. . ."

(The 47,000-square-foot plant is equipped to produce 240 million cans a year and has the capacity to store 12.5 million cans.)

The objective of brewers such as Schaefer and the can manufacturers is a simple one—increase the can production capability to meet the increasing consumer demand for canned beer, most of which is consumed in the home. Today, nearly 68 per cent of all beer purchased in the United States is consumed at home, quite a contrast to the 25 per cent total recorded in 1934, the year before the beer can made its appearance.

Packaging accounts for about 50 per cent of all brewing costs, according to Andrew J. Melnick, beer industry analyst for Drexel Burnham & Co. Inc., one of the leading international investment banking firms.

Melnick and other analysts see a growing trend toward in-plant manufacturing of beer cans by major U.S. brewers, chiefly because of the cost-savings factor involved in such production.

Lawrence J. Goldstein, vice president of Drexel Burnham, believes the entrance of the major brewers into the can-making field could serve as "a real bargaining point with the container manufacturers.

"It is estimated that can makers make substantial profits—about 25 per cent on their direct manufacturing costs. This would be available for recapture by the brewers," Goldstein said.

But despite the threat from the major brewers, the future looks solid for the nation's can makers, industry experts say.

U.S. beer production is expected to reach 150 million barrels (there are 31 gallons to a barrel, and per capita consumption was estimated at 20.1 gallons in 1973).

People are drinking more, and there are more of them.

"Beer and soft drinks, the fastest growing markets in the U.S., account for 47 per cent of total can shipments, compared with only 21.3 per cent in 1963," according to Standard and Poor's. Beer cans account for 47 per cent of that total.

In fact, the major growth area within the metal can industry has been convenience containers for beer and soft drinks. "Without the rapid development of these two markets, metal cans would have obtained only minimal growth at best," Standard and Poor's said.

Beer cans accounted for nine per cent of the industry's overall increase in can shipments in 1973. Despite the increased costs of raw materials, labor, freight, and fuel, and competition from glass containers and restrictive state legislation, shipments of metal cans are expected to increase about five to six percent annually during the

Paul DeMoss, Plant Manager of the Anheuser-Busch Jacksonville brewery, holds a display which shows the steps involved in making a two-piece can.
Photo courtesy Brewers Digest

next two or three years. Leading the way are the new two-piece, tin-free steel and aluminum cans being developed by the major can producers.

Let's look at the giants in the field.

American Can Company

The American Can Co., headquartered in Greenwich, Connecticut, recorded sales of $573 million in beverage packaging in 1973, producing nearly nine billion beer cans. Even the most optimistic American Can executive could not have foreseen such a staggering total when the company tip-toed onto the beverage packaging scene with its revolutionary Keglined beer can in 1935. That can—and those produced by American's competitors—eventually would change the course of both the can manufacturing and brewing industries. (The year before the beer can's introduction, 75 per cent of the beer sold in America was in draught form. The other 25 per cent was sold in returnable bottles.) More than 200 million beer cans were sold in 1935, mostly by American.

Total beer can production in the U.S. didn't reach the one billion mark until 1941, and American Can Co. accounted for the major share of that production. (In 1941, the last year of normal production prior to World War II, cans accounted for 14 per cent of total packaged beer sales; 186 of the nation's 507 licensed brewers were packaging their beer in cans.)

Why did American Can Co. pour millions of dollars into the development of the beer can, a long-shot gamble at best? The obvious answer: to make money. Can manufacturers—and the brewing industry—watched with considerable interest consumer demand following the repeal of Prohibition in 1933 for take-home containers for their beer. Explains an analyst:

"The trend was watched closely, particularly by the national-minded brewers who were seeking fast, profitable ways of renewing their franchises, establishing their brands in independently controlled retail outlets, and of broadening geographic range.

"The beer bottles of those days were mainly of 12-ounce and quart sizes. In wooden cases these were heavy, bulky, and fragile, and required deposits to assure their return. Cognizant of the brewers' problems, the American Can Company conceived the idea of a can for beer. Such a container would be light, compact, unbreakable, protect beer from air and light, eliminate deposits and returns, and be easily disposable."

And so a new era was born. A look at the types and varieties of beer cans produced by American Can Co. and the other can makers in 40 years, plus innovations provided by the various can manufacturers, will follow later in this chapter.

In 1974, American Can Co. had more than 60 plants in the U.S. and Canada producing steel and aluminum metal containers and metal specialties. (For a list of can plant locations, see Appendix II.)

The company, incorporated under the laws of New Jersey March 19, 1901, has general offices at American Lane, Greenwich, Connecticut 06830.

Continental Can Co.

Continental Can Co., headquartered in New York City, is the leading producer of containers in the U.S. It offers a diversified range of products and has major interests in metal, paper, and plastic packaging.

The company reported sales of more than $600 million in 1973, 42 per cent from it's metal operations (which accounted for 25 per cent of its income). Continental produced more than 8 billion beer cans in 1973, second to American Can Co.

It quickly followed American into producing cans for beer, introducing the cone or spout top wax-lined beer can in 1935, with its familiar "Cap-Sealed" trademark.

"It became apparent in the early 1930's that there would be a place for the convenient, one-way container for such things as beer, soft drinks, and motor oil," said Donald V. Earnshaw, vice president, office of public affairs, at Continental Can Co. "So Continental conducted extensive research on one-way containers and produced a variety of cans, including the cone top beer can (as an alternative to American's conventional flat top can, to serve brewers who found it impractical or financially unfeasible to switch to a process using the flat top can)."

Continental's cone top, which had a narrow spout similar to the one on a beer bottle, permitted the brewer (particularly the small local or regional brewer) to package cans by making minor modifications in his filling and capping equipment.

The Jos. Schlitz Brewing Co. of Milwaukee was the first brewer to use the cone top. It introduced beer in that container in September, 1935.

"But Continental's 'spout' can found its best reception with the small-to-medium-sized brewing companies, which did not have sufficient sales to warrant the high-volume oriented canning equipment sold by American," Robert Meyers observed in his history of the beer can.

"The big, national brewers were more interested in the flat-top cans (they could more easily afford the costly conversions to new filling machines), but most local brewers who began utilizing cans leaned toward the Continental's cone top," Mr. Earnshaw said.

Some 23 brewers began canning beer in 1935.

Continental Can Co.'s Metal Manufacturing Operating Division, headquartered in Chicago, operates 74 plants that manufacture beer cans and other metal containers, plus machinery for the beer, soft drink, wine, and distilled spirits industries.

It has facilities (in operation or under construction) with a capacity to produce more than 2 billion of its new two-piece beverage cans and has plans for an additional 2.5 billion-cans-per-year capacity by the end of 1975.

Incorporated in New York City on Jan. 17, 1913, Continental Can's general offices are at 633 Third Ave., New York, New York 10017

National Can Company

Ranking a distant third in annual beer can production, the Chicago-based National Can Co. produced about 2.9 billion beer cans in 1973. It reported sales in excess of $300 million.

National also jumped on the beer can band wagon in 1935 with a flat-top can similar to American's. But, unlike American, National was able to capture only a small share of the market.

It sold cans to only a few brewers in 1935-36, including the North-ampton Brewing Co. of Northampton, Pennsylvania, brewer of Tru-Blu and Tru-Blu White Seal.

While still maintaining its steel beer can production, National made a strong bid to garner a larger share of the aluminum can market in 1971 with heavy investments in new facilities to produce aluminum "drawn-and-ironed" cans. "This process was sub-sequently extended to steel cans, with the company presently having several facilities adaptable to both metals," a National spokesman said.

Incorporated in Delaware on Nov. 30, 1929, as the Metal Package Co. (changed to National Can Co. on April 1, 1935), National's general offices are at 5959 S. Cicero Ave., Chicago, Illinois 60638.

Reynolds Metals Company

Reynolds Metals, based in Richmond, Virginia, is the nation's leading producer of aluminum beer cans. In fact, aluminum cans are the only beer containers it produces.

In the early 1960's, Reynolds and the Aluminum Company of America (Alcoa) began producing easy-open, soft aluminum tops for beer cans. "Viewed primarily as a convenience feature, aluminum tops caught on quickly and were placed on most cans (produced) during the early 1960's," Mr. Meyers points out in his history of the can.

If the consumer and the brewing industry readily accepted aluminum tops on beer cans, why not all-aluminum cans? As early as 1959, the Adolph Coors Brewing Co. was making all-aluminum 7-ounce cans and was selling them with some success. So, the two major producers of aluminum products (chiefly aluminum foil, overwraps, and labels) developed all-aluminum, two-piece beer cans and introduced them in test markets in 1963. Reynolds Aluminum worked with the Hamm's Brewing Co. of St. Paul, Minnesota, in a Rockford, Illinois test, and Alcoa with Anheuser-Busch in the St. Louis area. The test sales proved successful and aluminum cans began making major inroads in the packaging fields.

Reynolds, with its 10 per cent share of the beer can market, manufactured nearly 2.5 billion beer cans in 1973.

Incorporated in Delaware on July 18, 1928, Reynolds Metals has corporate offices in the Reynolds Metals Building, Richmond, Virginia 23261.

Crown Cork & Seal Company

Crown, Cork & Seal Co., one of the major contributors to beer can technology, introduced its unique drawn-metal, wax-lined "Crowntainer" spout-top can in the early 1940's.

The Philadelphia-based company entered the beer can field with the purchase of the Acme Can Co. of that city. Its Crowntainer was shorter and wider than the then standard flat-top and cone-top cans produced by its competitors, had no side seam, and usually had silver coloring.

Crown, Cork & Seal produced more than 1.7 billion cans in 1973 and reported sales of $156 million. The fifth largest producer of beer cans now has nine lines, with the addition of three new ones during the last year. Each of the new lines is designed to produce about 150 million cans a year.

Crown, Cork & Seal Co. was incorporated in New York on Dec. 9, 1927, as the consolidation of the New Process Cork Co., Inc., and the New York Improved Patents Corp., which purchased the assets of the Crown, Cork & Seal Co. of Baltimore. It has corporate headquarters at 9300 Ashton Rd., Philadelphia, Pennsylvania 19136.

(The company also is the nation's leading manufacturer of caps and other metal closures for beer bottles and one of the top manufacturers of machinery to fill beer cans and bottles, electronic bottle inspection equipment, and bottle washers.)

Other Can Makers

Between the late 1930's and the early 1960's, beer cans also were produced by the Pacific Can Company of California ("Keglet", "Pacific Can", "Kan Keg"), Cans Inc. of Chicago, which merged with National Can Co. in 1953 ("Cans Inc."), Heekin Can Company of Cincinnati (a division of Diamond International), and Alcoa.

Beer Cans: Styles, Shapes, Sizes, Trademarks (1930's — 40's)

Throughout the colorful 40-year history of the beer can, there have

Mead 12-pack can packaging machine at the Queen City Brewing Co. This machine automatically sets up the carton and inserts 12 cans into it before sealing.

Photo courtesy Brewers Digest

been a wide assortment of styles, shapes, sizes, and trademarks. Each of these unique differences, large or small, have left their imprint on the beer packaging field. This section is devoted to the various innovations and changes introduced by the major can manufacturers. (Bob Myers provided a great deal of information contained in this section, including the comprehensive listing of beer can types at the end.)

American Can Company

Prior to the 1960's, American Can stuck to basic beer can designs, producing 12-ounce and 16-ounce flat top cans. However, to compete with Continental and Crown, American introduced its version of the 12-ounce spout top in the 1940's (it had a flat bottom). American also marketed a 32-ounce flat top and a quart spout can in the 1940's. However, in the mid-1950's, it redesigned the spout quart, retaining the bottle cap but considerably reducing the height of the spout so that it resembled a flat top.

When American Can introduced the flat top can in 1935, it also had to provide a method of opening the can. A bottle opener wouldn't open the new metal container, so American developed the "quick and easy opener" the "church key," a 5-inch piece of metal with a punch opener on one end and a bottle cap lifter on the other.

As an American Can Co. historian pointed out,

"Flat top cans could not have been as readily accepted without the development and wide distribution of an inexpensive and effective can opener.

"The original opener developed by American Can Company and later produced by the Vaughn Novelty Manufacturing Company . . . could be personalized with the brewer's name and were priced with discount at around a penny each.

"Initially, these were distributed through wholesalers and by insertion of one opener in each case of canned beer. It has been estimated that in order to saturate beer drinking homes, a quantity of openers equivalent to some 20 times the number of these homes needed to be put into wholesale and retail channels.

"During the 1950's, as a means of conserving raw material, give-away openers were reduced in length to about 3 inches. . .

"In a national survey conducted in 1967, some four years after the introduction of self-opening ends ("pop top" or "pull top" cans marketed by Alcoa that did not require a can opener), 98 per cent of American homes were equipped with punch openers. . ."

Continental Can Company

Continental's introduction of the spout or cone top can has been discussed in detail elsewhere in this chapter. We should point out, however, that there were two varieties of the Continental Cap-Sealed cone top.

One model was a low-profile can with a shorter spout. This can had sides that measured 4-5/8 inches high and a 3/4-inch spout.

The other version was a high-profile can, with sides that measured 4 1/2 inches and a 1 1/8-inch spout.

Bob Meyers points out that "the height of the spout is a quick clue to the age of a Continental cone top. All pre-World War II spouts by Continental have a low profile, compared to those used during and after the war, which were higher.

In addition, Continental spout tops produced in late 1935 and during the first half of 1936 had flat bottoms and had an unvarnished top (which, he points out, rusted quickly).

The Continental spout tops were made in 12-, 16- and 32-ounce sizes, the latter after 1938.

During the mid-1940's, Continental introduced its flat top, which also carried the familiar "Cap-Sealed" trademark. (A complete description of trademark changes is given later in this chapter.)

Following World War II, there was a steady drift toward the flat top can by most brewers, and the cone top was traveling the road toward eventual extinction. ("By the late 1940's, the convenience factor of the flat-top cans—they were easier for the merchant and consumer to store—was beginning to outweigh the economic factor for the brewer, large and small, according to Donald Earnshaw of Continental.)

Crown Cork & Seal Company

Crown Cork & Seal Co. produced both flat and spout top cans, but it is most noted for both its unusual spout top (introduced in the early 1940's) and perhaps the widest variety of cans produced in the U.S.

The squat "Crowntainer" was of three-piece construction: a seamless side, a bottom, and a cap. It has no welded seams or tops like the Continental, American, and National cans.

The "Crowntainer," which featured some of the most colorful and masterfully designed labels (used by many Midwestern and Eastern brewers), was constructed of tinless "black plate" covered with powdered aluminum, which gave it its distinct silver color.

Crown's spout top stood only 5 inches high, considerably shorter than Continental's high-profile can. (The standard flat top can of the period was about 4-3/4 inches tall.)

"Crown's other unique spout design, also begun before the war," Bob Myers points out, "had an odd shaped spout—the portion ending in the bottle cap was quite elongated compared to other spouts."

Prior to the war, Crown also produced quart spouts, and 8- and 12-

ounce flat tops. But in 1946, the company began producing a spout top similar to Continental's high-profile model and an odd-looking flat top that was taller and slimmer than the conventional 12-ounce models.

"After trying these very individualistic shapes, the only (Crown) can that survived was the usual flat top. Maybe (if there were) more can collectors back then, the 'can lobby' could have encouraged these most-collectible can types to be made longer," Mr. Myers mused in his study of the can.

The Crowntainer did survive until the early 1950's.

National Can Co. and a number of smaller companies also were producing cans at this time, but they were of the traditional flat-top style.

It also should be noted that because of the demands on metal supplies created by the war effort, can production was sharply curtailed between 1941 and 1946. Although restrictions on the use of tinplate all but eliminated beer cans from the domestic market during the war years, more than 1 billion cans of beer were shipped overseas to American armed forces, young men who were the principal consumers of beer.

According to an American Can Co. study:

"In a survey conducted in 1947, six years after advertising (of canned beer) had been discontinued, 38 per cent of beer drinkers were still able to correctly identify the trademark "Keglined" and canned beer usage was found to be significantly higher (by 32 per cent) in veteran than non-veteran homes."

"World War II turned the tide for beer cans," said Continental Can's Mr. Earnshaw. "GI's drank a billion cans of beer and they liked it. Their preference for canned beer significantly heightened the demand for the product after the war."

The 1950's—Farewell Cone Top

The changing post-war world of the 1950's brought about new lifestyles in the U.S., some spawned by great advances in American industrial technology.

One of the victims of these changing times was the venerable cone or spout-top can, which had fallen in disfavor with brewers and merchants. As Bob Myers comments:

"During the early to middle 1950's, Continental's "Cap-Sealed" can began losing ground to the various flat-top cans. Many breweries were increasing in size, which put greater emphasis on packaging-line speed, and the "Cap-Sealed" can could not be filled as fast as its competitor (the same held true for the "Crowntainer"). Retailers complained about the difficulty in making display stacks with the spout cans. Furthermore, opening the flat-top cans had become an accepted operation, thus diminishing the advantage the "Cap-Sealed" can once had by looking and opening like the familiar bottle."

Given the amount of opposition to the spout top, Continental and Crown Cork & Seal stopped promoting and marketing the obsolete container in the 1950's. Mr. Earnshaw also offers an interesting theory on the fadeout of the cone top: "The major national brewers were all using flat-top cans by the 1950's, and they were beginning to advertise on a broad scale throughout the United States. Most beer consumers identified with the flat-top can used by the major brewers and tended to look down on the few local and regional brands packaged in cone tops."

The 1950's also witnessed the brewing and can-making industries' introduction of the aluminum can and their departure from the conventional 12- and 32-ounce can sizes. Appearing on the packaging scene were the 16-ounce flat-top cans (first introduced by Schlitz in June, 1954, in an effort to regain the share of the beer market it lost during the bitter strike at its Milwaukee brewery in 1953), flat-top quart cans (distributed by the P. Ballantine Brewing Co. in 1956), and the diminutive 8-ounce cans used by the Goebel and Goetz brewing companies.

But these changes—actually relatively minor cosmetic alterations—were but a modest prelude to the innovative 1960's just over the horizon.

The 1960's—Changes by the Caseload

The 1960's also were marked by a changing mood in American society—a desire to leave the well-worn past far behind. This mood also prevailed in industry. There was little choice but to accept it, for industry in the U.S. and throughout the world was being revolutionized by great leaps forward in technology on just about every front. The growing phenomenon of space technology (remember the "Sputnik" shock?) and the adaptations of that new generation of technological advances to domestic uses was pushing industry into a new world, a world with seemingly unlimited possibilities for new products and uses for materials.

It also was the beginning of a new era of consumer awareness and demands for more convenience in just about every product line—from washing machines and automobiles to kitchen appliances and. . .yes. . .to beverage packaging.

Easy-open end:

For some beer drinkers (and soft-drink devotees), getting through the solid steel top of a can with an opener was a genuine struggle. The aluminum companies recognized this problem and in late 1959 and early 1960 introduced a soft-top aluminum end that was light and easy to open.

Promoted initially by Schlitz as the "Softop" can, it still had a tinplate body and bottom and required a can opener. But it was a big step toward providing increased convenience for the consumer.

The "Tab Top":

Alcoa and the Pittsburgh Brewing Co. dropped the real blockbuster on the packaging industry in 1962 when they introduced a can that required no opener. The lift tab—a small piece of metal that the consumer ripped in a zipper-like fashion to open the can—was developed by Ermal C. Fraze, owner of the Dayton Reliable Tool Co. of Dayton, Ohio. He then sold exclusive rights to the tab top and other easy-open design patents to Alcoa.

Pittsburgh Brewing Co. marketed its Iron City brand (carrying the promotion: "New Easy Open Snap Top") in a test market in Virginia to determine if it had a saleable container.

"The market test conducted in Virginia was watched closely by brewers and can suppliers; and the new end was judged to be an interesting development, but perhaps not worth the additional packaging cost," an American Can Co. spokesman observed.

In February, 1963, Schlitz introduced the new lift tab top end on a national scale with extensive television, newspaper, magazine, and billboard advertising.

But while the lift tab was fairly well received by consumers, it left much to be desired when it came to safety. Many of the tops were difficult to open and, in some cases, consumers slashed a finger or knuckle trying to pry open a stubborn tab top. But most beer drinkers didn't seem to mind the perils of opening cans.

"The consumer apparently was perfectly delighted to cut his finger once a six-pack and come back for more," said Continental's Mr. Earnshaw.

And come back they did. The early marketing efforts by Pittsburgh Brewing and Schlitz were so successful that by July, 1963, 40 brands were on the market with lift tabs, and nearly 70 brands by September of the same year. By 1965, more than 70 per cent of all beer cans were easy-open aluminum cans; more than 90 per cent were in 1970; and nearly 100 per cent were in 1975.

The major can companies, quick to realize that the lift tab top was here to stay, sharply increased production to meet the growing demand for the tabs. They also worked to develop improved tab top designs.

Following the original and rather crude lift top can came the U-tab, which had folded-in edges and was easier and safer to open. Then came "Ring Pull" in 1965—another Fraze invention. It replaced the stubby tab and provided greater ease of opening and safety. The ring later was given "dimples" to make it even easier to lift.

The can companies also made progressive improvements on the pouring aperture, the "hole" on top of the can.

Continental's "Ring Pull" aluminum end and American's "Touch 'n Go" end have dominated the market since the late 1960's.

Aluminum Cans:

Coors began using aluminum on the tops of its beer cans in the late 1950's and introduced its all-aluminum 7-ounce can in 1959 in its Western market. Then came Reynold's Hamm's can and Alcoa's Budweiser and Busch Bavarian cans in 1963. It was not until 1964, however, that a number of other brands appeared in all-aluminum cans in test markets.

The main selling points of the two-piece aluminum can (constructed from a single disk of aluminum, with the top added after filling) were its light weight and ability to chill quickly. The brewer's label also reproduced extremely well on aluminum cans.

With minor modifications, aluminum cans would run on existing canning lines. This provided brewers with an alternative source of supply in a sometimes unstable metal market.

By 1967, nearly 10 per cent of all beer cans sold were aluminum; by 1974, that figure had more than doubled. Today, more than 1 billion pounds of aluminum annually is used to make aluminum cans and can ends.

These innovations and other can-making advancements were closing the book on the traditional three-piece soldered, steel can by the late 1960's. Let's look at some of those new techniques.

Tin Free Steel (TFS):

Aggressive marketing by the aluminum companies forced the major can-makers to develop alternative materials for their beer cans.

In the early 1960's, National announced that it had developed a low-cost composite can made of tin-plated steel foil as an alternative to the three-piece heavy steel can. The can never was placed on the commercial market.

The major technological change in this area came later in the decade with the introduction of the tin-free steel (TFS) can. It replaced the traditional tin coating on cans with a less expensive and durable chemical coating. By 1969, American had shipped more than 3 billion tin-free steel cans to brewers.

In addition to shifts to new materials, the can companies developed new assembly methods—glueing or welding three-piece cans instead of soldering them.

"Mira Seam" and "Conoweld":

American Can Co. began shifting to tin-free steel in the late 1960's after successfully developing an adhesive cement to bond the can seams. The company introduced the innovative container on the market under the trademark "Mira Seam." American announced development of the method in 1965.

American heralded the development with a strong advertising campaign in brewing industry trade publications, calling it "the impossible seam." As one ad pointed out:

"Nobody loves a wide seam. Until now the only way to join the familiar household can was to solder it. This produced a very wide seam and made all-around label decorations impossible.

(Mira Seam) is a bonding process using a specially developed thermoplastic adhesive, equivalent to that used in the Apollo Space Program. . .(and) since Mira Seam is a bonding and not a soldering process, tin is no longer needed on steel as a fusing agent. This substantially reduces the cost of metal cans to the beverage industry."

Shortly after American's marketing of its "Mira Seam" cans, Continental began making solderless cans under the trademark 'Conoweld." But instead of joining its can parts with an adhesive like American, Continental used an electric welding process.

Both methods eliminated the somewhat crude, wide side-seam from the cans, permitting the lithographing of a brewer's label almost completely around the can.

The 1960's provided such significant innovations as drawn and ironed cans, two-piece all-aluminum, and tin-free steel cans with welded or cemented seams, but the 1970's have been providing even broader advancements in can technology.

The 1970's: Era of the Two-Piece Can

With little question, the most significant technological advancement in the can industry in the first four years of the 1970's is the development and widespread use of the drawn and ironed, two-piece, seamless can similar to the familiar existing aluminum can.

In the manufacture of the seamless, two-piece can, the aluminum alloy or steel in sheet form is fed into a press, where it is blanked and shaped into cups. The cup is then fed into an ironing press where the diameter is reduced and the side wall is ironed to reduce the gauge and achieve the necessary can height.

Thus, the two-piece can has only a body and a top that's added after the can is filled.

"Beer can technology is firmly centered on the two-piece can," according to Continental's Mr. Earnshaw. "It's the can of the future."

In 1972, more than 8 billion two-piece cans were produced, or

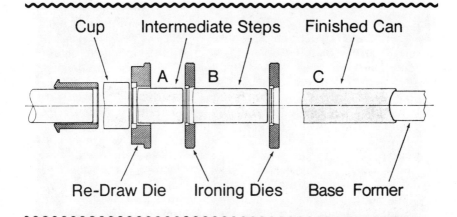

Schematic shows stages in manufacture of drawn & ironed can.
[*Reprinted with permission from* Modern Metals Magazine.)

about 25 per cent of all beverage cans manufactured that year. "This growth . . . is expected to rise sharply by 1976, with the percentage of two-piece units predicted to rise to about 50 per cent," according to one can company spokesman.

Among the two-piece cans' advantages are: (1) They use less steel than other beverage containers, (2) they possess good magnetic collection and recycling properties, (3) they don't need to undergo alloy separation, and (4) they require less energy to process the raw material for the steel container.

Other innovations that have appeared on the packaging scene in the last four years—thanks mainly to advancements such as two-piece construction and cemented and welded seams—are necked-in cans (crimps on sides of newer lightweight three-piece cans where the sides meet the top and bottom) and stylized cans, such as the keg-shaped Hamms can.

"And because of the recent technological advancements, can companies have been able to produce a variety of can shapes—keg- or barrel-shaped, pear-shaped, and hourglass-shaped," Mr. Earnshaw said. "However, the per unit cost of the stylized cans, in most cases, is higher than conventional cans, and that factor could limit the demand for that type of can," he added.

Another significant innovation of the 1970's is American Can Company's "Button Down End" opener for beer and soft drink cans. The new opening—two "Buttons" on the top of the can, one for venting and the other for pouring—may eventually replace the tab top opener on cans.

Metal Container Corp., a subsidiary of Anheuser-Busch, Inc. has developed a production control system with on-line computers producing 2.5 million cans daily.

Photo courtesy Brewers Digest

American Can claims its button end is safer, more convenient, and will not contribute to this country's already serious litter problem like the tab tops (the buttons are pushed under the can's lid by the drinker's finger and remain attached to the can).

The new tops, which can be placed on both steel and aluminum cans, are being tested in a number of U.S. markets (mainly in the West and Southwest) by, most notably, Anheuser Busch, Coors, and Blitz-Wienhard of Portland Oregon.

The Beer Can's Future

Despite competition from bottles (both the familiar glass variety and new plastic bottles being developed and tested in the U.S. and Eurqpe), anti-can laws and opposition from ecologists, and futuristic "cans" (such as the curious-looking, stiff-paper, sachet-type container called "Merolite," that was developed by the Imperial Chemical Industries, Ltd., and Watney Mann Ltd., brewers, both of London, England), can makers are confident that the can as millions of consumers know it has a bright future.

As Continental Can's Donald Earnshaw puts it, with strong conviction: "Cans will be a dominant factor in consumer packaging for a long, long time."

Further thoughts on the beer can's future will be discussed in Chapter 12.

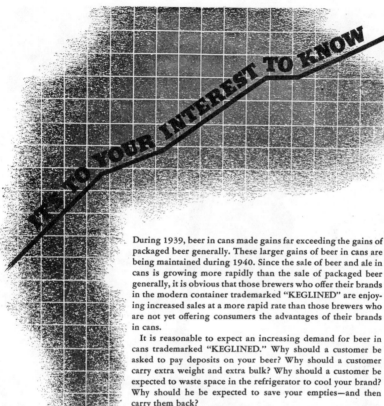

IT'S TO YOUR INTEREST TO KNOW

During 1939, beer in cans made gains far exceeding the gains of packaged beer generally. These larger gains of beer in cans are being maintained during 1940. Since the sale of beer and ale in cans is growing more rapidly than the sale of packaged beer generally, it is obvious that those brewers who offer their brands in the modern container trademarked "KEGLINED" are enjoying increased sales at a more rapid rate than those brewers who are not yet offering consumers the advantages of their brands in cans.

It is reasonable to expect an increasing demand for beer in cans trademarked "KEGLINED." Why should a customer be asked to pay deposits on your beer? Why should a customer carry extra weight and extra bulk? Why should a customer be expected to waste space in the refrigerator to cool your brand? Why should he be expected to save your empties—and then carry them back?

Why should a beer drinker do all these things—when he can buy beer in cans trademarked "KEGLINED"? Why, in short, shouldn't you ride with the trend—ride with the *greater gains* of beer and ale *in cans?*

More than 7 out of every 10 people who buy beer or ale in cans—buy it in cans trademarked "KEGLINED." Perhaps you should have a serious talk, now, with a representative of the American Can Company.

Increase profits, reduce expense with beer and ale in cans trademarked "KEGLINED." The better brands come this better way. Order from your supplier today.

AMERICAN CAN COMPANY
230 Park Avenue, New York

TODAY'S TRENDS ARE TOMORROW'S FACTS

Today's trends are tomorrow's facts. Ever since the American Can Company introduced the can for beer and ale—the trend has been toward cans. In 1936, approximately 500,000,000 cans of beer and ale were consumed . . . in 1940, that number will be more than 800,000,000 cans.

Let us look behind this 60% rise. The advent of cans has undoubtedly made beer buying easier.

It is self-evident that the more obstacles placed in the way of the consumer, the more likely you will find sales resistance. These obstacles have been completely removed by cans. They have removed the need of paying deposits—they have made beer easier to carry by reducing weight and bulk—they have made beer more welcome in the home because they can be stacked compactly in

e refrigerator—they have eliminated the need f saving and carrying back empties. Cans have mplified beer buying for the consumer—just as ey have simplified beer handling for the retailer.

Upon these proven values, the American Can ompany has designed and built its national advertising campaign to consumers. Each adverement dramatizes, realistically, how cans trademarked "KEGLINED" simplify the consumer's eer and ale buying. This consumer advertising, ow appearing in America's important weekly nd monthly magazines, supplements the nation-wide promotion of beer and ale in cans to America's 328,000 licensed retailers. On every important front, the American Can Company continues to promote the container preferred by 7 out of every 10 consumers who buy beer in cans, knowing that the trend toward cans is based upon sound values.

Brewers whose brands are not yet in cans trademarked "KEGLINED" should be interested in this trend.

It might be advisable to talk it over with a representative of the American Can Co.

MERICAN CAN COMPANY · 230 PARK AVENUE · NEW YORK

ENOUGH BEER TO FLOAT THE QUEEN MARY

If all the beer sold in cans marked "Keglined" were poured into one mighty stein, there would be enough beer to float the Queen Mary, with enough left over for the tugs it takes to dock her. . . It's this amazing volume that is back of the decision of brewer after brewer to adopt this can.

PRODUCT OF

AMERICAN CAN COMPANY

230 PARK AVE. CANCO NEW YORK

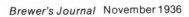

Continental Can Company Stages Big Summer Drive

IN PROMOTING ITS BIG SUM-mer campaign, Continental Can Company makes a point that of the 30 million cases of canned beer sold in 1939, 6½ million were disposed of in July and August alone. With a strong assurance that 1940 sales would exceed 1939, the company stresses the significance that retail outlets, backed by the company's special promotion, and the help of the 83 breweries using Cap-Sealed cans, would find this extra big volume all PLUS business "because it does not affect bottle sales."

There is good psychology back of that stand—for the retailer of any merchandise is interested in sales cooperation that gives him plus business. There isn't any point in promoting one item at the expense of another—as BREWERS JOURNAL has stressed in its campaign to save the draught beer business, showing that sales of package beer would profit too.

The Continental summer coopera-tive plan has been backed by some most effective advertising. One of these is reproduced here. These ads (there are nine of them) are all double-spreads, so placed in widely read magazines that they cover every city, town and hamlet. They are being continued through August and early September. Thus each dealer has the benefit of advertising that is local. Such advertising is not only attractive, but compelling.

Continental Can Company has also put a bonus-incentive plan into operation that has proven to be a sales stimulant beyond expecta-tions. Thousands of distributors' salesmen were keyed up to the de-sirability of increasing the sale of beer in Cap-Sealed cans, in view of the fact that prizes are in cash. Everyone is interested in earnings increase—and that, too, is good psy-chology.

The recent spell of hot weather has been a great aid in making this campaign effective, particularly in view of the fact that the double-spread advertising in Life, Collier's and Liberty has stressed the con-venience of Cap-Sealed cans for pic-nics, outings, parties, and many other occasions.

Altogether, this has the ear-marks of the type of sales promo-tion that helps to increase total beer sales, rather than being sim-ply competitive. Beer and ale are referred to as "the ideal summer beverages"—and that is good sales copy.

Advertisement that appeared in Life and other magazines in July

3500 DISTRIBUTORS CAN'T BE WRONG!

NATION-WIDE SURVEY REVEALS NEW FACTS ABOUT CANNED BEER AND THE CAP-SEALED CAN...

Canned beer is going to hit a new high this year! Leading distributors from coast to coast—3500 strong—say so. Their sales for the first eight months of 1940 prove it. How does Continental know? Continental asked. Not by letter, not by telephone, not by telegraph ... but by personal calls made by our own men. These men, covering the 48 states of the nation last summer, conducted the greatest marketing and merchandising survey ever made among America's beer distributors. They learned that ...

CANNED BEER BUSINESS IS BETTER THAN EVER

Sales of canned beer are already exceeding the record set in 1939. Of the distributors answering the poll, 1,797 said their sales were ahead, or equal to last year's. Only 332 said they were behind. Further evidence of the gaining popularity of canned beer is found right in Continental's own sales records. Continental's shipments of Cap-Sealed cans at the end of the summer were 30 PER CENT ahead of last year!

DISTRIBUTORS PREFER THE CAP-SEALED CAN

Distributors were also asked this question— "Which do you prefer, the Cap-Sealed can or the flat-top can?" Here's the vote:—2,032 said they preferred the Cap-Sealed can, 102 said their choice was the flat-top can, 232 had no particular choice. Why this overwhelming preference? The sale of Cap-Sealed cans is a clean-cut, one-way transaction, with no special openers to bother with. Moreover, distributors want the can that's the popular choice of every two out of three beer drinkers. Continental's consumer surveys in city after city throughout the country have always shown that the Cap-Sealed can is *the* choice.

DISTRIBUTORS LIKE CONTINENTAL'S PROMOTION

They were enthusiastic about Continental's powerful advertising campaign all summer in LIFE, LIBERTY, and COLLIER'S. But best of all they liked the local sales promotion support given

CONTINENTAL CAN COMPANY

them right in their own territory, a combination which they said helped to build their package sales and volume.

PROMOTION BUILDS NEW BUSINESS

Brewers like Continental's well-rounded promotion support too. Throughout the country, more brewers are packing their beer and ale in Cap-Sealed cans than in any other beer can made. And this year, so far, 19 more brewers have adopted Continental's Cap-Sealed can.

★   ★   ★

MORE MARKETING INFORMATION FOR YOU

As a result of this intensive campaigning, Con-

tinental has more complete information on the marketing and merchandising of canned beer than ever before in its history. This vital information, gathered throughout all 48 states, is available to brewers interested in increasing their package beer sales. We'll be glad to show you in detail how it will pay you to join the many other successful users of the 12-ounce and the 32-ounce Cap-Sealed cans.

Continental Crowns are the choice of leading brewers and bottlers today. Why? Because we can supply quality Crowns, spotted or plain, in any quantity without delay. And you can count on them just as you can count on the Cap-Sealed can.

Covering the

Continental Can

Country !

BEER

CANS

. . . now sold in 45 states

THREE MONTHS AGO there were no beers or ales in Cap Sealed Cans. Today there are ten, and many more on the way. Three months ago you couldn't buy beer in this new container anywhere. Today it is sold in 45 states.

Why this sudden growth? Simply because brewers and distributors have discovered in the Cap Sealed Can all the advantages of cans for beer, plus a bottle-like ease of filling, opening, pouring, or drinking.

Said one well-known brewer, "After months of careful research and continuous testing in our laboratories, our scientists and brewmasters are satisfied that they have found, in the Continental Cap Sealed Can, a container that has all the requirements—all the advantages and safeguards that they have insisted upon before offering our beer in this new and modern type of container."

In practically every case where the Cap Sealed Can has been adopted, sales increases have been sensational. One distributor had a boost of 200 per cent in a week.

Why not cash in on this country-wide demand for beer put up this modern way?

*   *   *

ADVANTAGES OF BEER IN CAP SEALED CANS . . . Protected from light . . . No deposits, no returns . . . Easier to handle . . . No extra loss of carbonization . . . Less oxygen trapped in sealing . . . Special lining, put in after can is made, protects flavor . . . Cuts pasteurizing time . . . Cuts storage space in half . . . No soaking, no labeling . . . Cuts delivery cost in half.

Company

NEW YORK

CHICAGO   SAN FRANCISCO

So now it's going to be

Collier's for October 5th, 1935

Continental Can Announces
BEER

A·h·h·h

in CAP SEALED

BEER

USE ANY BOTTLE OPENER

Tastes better • Easy to open
Protected from light
No deposit • No empties to return
Cools quicker • Takes up less space
No danger of breakage
Sanitary—used once—thrown away
Holds 12 fluid ounces same as bottle
Drink right from can if you wish

Continental

Can Company

Above is reproduced a two-page advertisement of Continental Can Company that appears in Time on Sept. 16; New Yorker, Sept. 21; Collier's, Oct. 5; Fortune, November; and Esquire, November.

CONTINENTAL
NEW YORK   CHICAGO

BEER *in* CANS

ier's for October 6th, 1935.

CANS

Now you're going to know what fine beer really ought to taste like — right in your own home or anywhere.

A brand-new container makes it possible... a special can designed by Continental Can Company after long research. This can is sealed with a cap and opens just like a bottle.

There are many reasons why you will prefer beer in this handy new container. But the chief reason is that it tastes better. Why is this?

Because the can permits faster pasteurization. Because it keeps out flavor-robbing light. because Continental's special lining re--the brewery goodness unchanged.

present we can't make these cans fast to keep up with demand. But before should be able to enjoy your favorite this new and better container. Watch k for it — and you'll thank us.

NOTICE TO BREWERS

have been pleased to learn that al's cap-sealed can may be run t bottling lines with very little quipment. Full details on request.

NEW YORK
O   SAN FRANCISCO

O NCE MORE a great industry is being revolutionized.

Yesterday it was canned oil—and millions of motorists changed their buying habit. Today it is canned beer—and millions of beer lovers are changing their drinking habit.

Starting at once, the Continental Can Company is launching a powerful advertising campaign in national magazines, telling the public why beer is so much better in Continental's new Cap Sealed Can that opens like a bottle and protects against light.

The first advertisement in this campaign is reproduced here. It will be followed by other full-page advertisements appearing regularly in the magazines shown at the left.

As a progressive leader of the can industry, Continental believes in cooperating with its customers. As a brewer who knows an opportunity when he sees one, you will want to get in touch with us.

CAN COMPANY
SAN FRANCISCO

4 more

LEADING BREWERS
JOIN THE PARADE

YOU may judge this Cap Sealed Can by the company it keeps. To the list of leading brewers who already have adopted the Cap Sealed Can for their beer, we now add four more: the Minneapolis Brewing Co. of Minneapolis, Rainier Brewing Company of San Francisco, Gluek Brewing Company of Minneapolis, and El Rey Brewing Company of San Francisco.

They all chose this can for its exclusive qualities. It opens and pours as easily as a bottle—from a cap-protected surface. The lining, applied *after* the can is made, gives perfect protection to the beer's flavor.

Why not march on to new and profitable markets with the Cap Sealed Can?

Continental Can Company

NEW YORK   CHICAGO   SAN FRANCISCO

OPENING UP A BIGGER SUMMER MARKET FOR BEER

For years, people have wished for beer in a compact, light-weight container—easy to take on picnics and other outdoor trips.

The Cap Can gives people what they want—not merely compact and quick-chilling, but easy to open, easy to pour—easy to drink from.

A carton holds a case; half the weight—half the space. Handy—no deposits to pay—no empties to return.

—and Brewers using cap cans will get the major part of this increased summer business

Ads like this, in national magazines and newspaper magazine sections, are getting the story over to millions of beer drinkers.

..it's a picnic

wherever you are, Beer in Cap Sealed Cans

BEER in CAP SEALED CANS

Continental Can Company

Continental Can Company

· NEW YORK · CHICAGO · SAN FRANCISCO

On the streets of 20 cities from coast to coast, unbiased reporters stopped people on the street, held out two beer cans, asked "WHICH CAN DO YOU PREFER?"

2 to 1 the nation voted for the Cap Sealed Can

WE wanted to find out which type of beer can is preferred by the public. So we turned the job over to a company that makes a business of conducting such surveys. They covered 20 cities. The Cap Sealed Can was a 2 to 1 choice.

How did that happen? Let's take a look at the reasons people gave for their preference: "Easier to open"..."Easier to pour"..."Can use any type opener"... "Can drink from can"..."Doesn't spill."

Every one of their reasons was based upon the features that make the difference between the Cap Sealed Can and flat top cans. And remember—these were the opinions of people who said they serve beer in their homes.

This national vote is worth a lot to brewers. If you haven't yet decided whether or not to put your beer in cans —or if you have been figuring out which can to use—the "voice of beer drinkers" can help you decide.

THE REASONS THEY GAVE

The reasons people gave for their choice of the Cap Sealed Can are:

"Easier to open" . . . "Easier to pour" . . . "Can use any type opener" . . . "Can drink from can" . . . "Doesn't spill."

Beer drinkers enjoy these **features** only with the Cap Sealed Can.

Continental Can Company
NEW YORK · CHICAGO · SAN FRANCISCO

SEND FOR YOUR FREE COPY OF "THE BEER DRINKER SPEAKS." IT TELLS THE COMPLETE STORY OF THE SURVEY

THE CAN THAT IS *made for beer!*

The Cap Sealed Can isn't just an ordinary can adapted for beer. From top to bottom, it is specially designed to deliver beer in perfect condition.

OPENS EASILY AND POURS CLEANLY

THE Cap Sealed Can comes to the brewer *complete*, ready for filling and capping. The final lining is applied *after* the can is made. This is insurance that your beer reaches the public with all its brewery goodness intact.

There isn't a flat surface to this can. From its concave bottom to its sloping reinforced-rib top, it is proportioned for strength. It stands the strains and pressure of pasteurization without "giving" or causing the lining to loosen.

The public are sold on the Cap Sealed Can. They like the way beer tastes in it. And they like the ease and convenience of a can that opens and pours smoothly—from a clean, protected surface.

Why not, right now, choose the can that has all these exclusive advantages . . . the can that is backed by Continental's extensive advertising and merchandising campaign . . . the Cap Sealed Can?

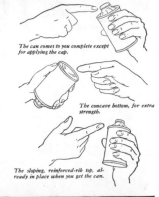

The can comes to you complete except for applying the cap.

The concave bottom, for extra strength.

The sloping, reinforced-rib top, already in place when you get the can.

Continental Can Company

NEW YORK • CHICAGO • SAN FRANCISCO

Why We Designed
A *Special* Can For Beer

CONTINENTAL wasn't first to put a beer can on the market. But when the Cap Sealed Can was introduced, it was a *beer can*. You couldn't possibly put tomatoes in it, and it wouldn't be right for soup. It is specially made for beer. How? By combining the best features of both the bottle and the can. It offers beer drinkers the most convenience.

They can even drink from this can if they want to, without any fear, because the pouring and drinking surface is completely protected by the cap. No special opener is needed, and the contents can't spout any more than a bottle.

As to what the public thinks about it — a nation-wide survey shows consumer preference for Cap Sealed Cans by a vote of nearly 3 to 1. It pays to sell folks what they want. • • •

Dealers are interested in the way canned beer can be displayed. Cap Sealed Brews not only lend themselves perfectly to "jumbled" displays in baskets or boxes on the counter, but make slide-proof built up displays. Illustration below shows the 4-can unit that can be combined into a display of any reasonable height.

Continental Can Company

NEW YORK • CHICAGO • SAN FRANCISCO

THEY'VE QUIT FIGHTING OVER BEER BOTTLES vs. CANS

THE CAP SEALED CAN . . . SPECIALLY MADE FOR BEER . . . COMBINES THE BEST POINTS OF BOTTLE AND CAN

IT was a hot argument while it lasted. Some folks thought they preferred beer in bottles. Others liked beer in cans. But along came the Cap Sealed Can. And now the public is happy, for this *custom-built* beer container embodies the best features of both can and bottle.

For instance, the Cap Sealed Can opens and pours just like a beer bottle. You can drink right out of the can, from a clean, cap-protected, sanitary opening. Yet the beer has all of the original delicious brewery flavor. That's because it is protected from light; pasteurized quicker, and the can, like a beer barrel, is lined *after* it is made to insure a one-piece lining.

On summer outings you'll like the way the Cap Sealed Can chills quickly . . . saves you half the weight of deposits and eliminates the problem of breakage. In fact, it . . . does away with breakage. As beer on any occasion. To make sure of getting the finest beer in the finest container, ask for the Cap Sealed Can.

Continental Can Company

THE ADVANTAGES OF THE FAMILIAR BOTTLE . . . easy to open . . . easy to drink . . . convenient to pour . . . the beer pours from . . . the cap-protected opening . . . clean, cap-protected opening.

WITH ALL THE ADVANTAGES OF THE CAN . . . saves half the weight and deposits . . . no deposits . . . cools quickly . . . easy to return . . . can't break . . . empties to return . . . can't break.

THIS campaign is running right now, when the beer season is at its peak, large size space, in local newspapers all over the country. Also tie-in advertising of beers in Cap Sealed Cans is running on the same page. This can't help making people want beer in the Cap Sealed Can. If they demand *your* beer that way, will they be able to get it?

CONSUMER MILLIONS..

Gain the ENJOYMENT and PROTECTION of BEER and ALE in "NATIONAL" DOUBLE-LINED NON-REFILLABLE CANS

"NATIONAL"

• ONE OF AMERICA'S LARGEST CANMAKERS •

NATIONAL CAN CO., 'INC' • EXECUTIVE OFFICES 110 EAST 42nd STREET • NEW YORK CITY

NEW BRANDS

by "COMMONWEALTH"

CLIMAXING features of healthfulness and superlative flavor with the definite PROTECTIVE assurance of

DOUBLE-LINED

TRADE MARK REGISTERED

non-refillable CANS

A Packaging achievement by "NATIONAL"—the mainspring to widened markets for Beer and Ale.

"NATIONAL"

NATIONAL CAN CO., 'INC' · EXECUTIVE OFFICES · 110 E. 42nd ST. · NEW YORK CITY

Brewer's Journal July 1936

Parade of the
"NATIONAL" GUARD!

YOUR PROTECTOR in Competition Battle . . . invincible ally in sales offense . . . packaged preference of American Dealer Legion . . . the pageant of NATIONAL **DOUBLE-LINED** NON-REFILLABLE CANS sweeps on to victory. ● New recruits constantly joining . . . Enlist now . . . Go NATIONAL !

AND NOW COMES

Tapster

THE SERVICE
FOR
BEER-IN-CANS

"OPENS
as it
SHUTS"

A Product of
REVERE COPPER & BRASS, INC.,
Rome, N. Y.

"NATIONAL"
NATIONAL CAN COMPANY, 'INC.' ● Executive Offices, 110 E. 42nd St., N. Y.

APPEARANCE
in Beer Cans
DOES COUNT...

BEER is on display . . . all dressed up and going places. This year, sales of packaged beer have reached the amazing figure of 38% of the total.

The new CCS Cans for beer take full advantage of this trend. Taller, slimmer and well proportioned, they have the smartness and "eye appeal" which invites the public to buy. Their modern, streamlined appearance gives your brand an air of distinction that suggests a finer brew

Keep pace with packaging progress and this new sales trend in the brewing industry. Your nearest CCS Office will give you full information.

CROWN CORK AND SEAL COMPANY

CAN DIVISION

BALTIMORE, MD.
PHILADELPHIA, PA.
(ACME CAN CO.)

THE *Ultra-Modern* CONTAINER FOR BEER

In the CROWNTAINER, Crown Engineers have pioneered an entirely new container for beer. This streamlined can is made without top seam or side seam. It is literally a steel bottle, protected with an aluminum coating and may be beautifully decorated in color.

In addition to giving the CROWNTAINER a striking appearance, the streamlining also has a very practical effect — it facilitates the exhaustion of air from the head space during the filling operation. But the ease with which beer may be poured from this smart, new container is one of its chief appeals to consumers.

On the inside, the CROWNTAINER is sprayed with a heavy lining of Crown's exclusive "Fermax", making it entirely neutral as to taste and odor. Because there is no side seam, a smooth, even coating is achieved which provides keeping qualities for beer unequalled in other metal packages.

A number of prominent breweries have contracted for the entire output of the first production unit at Philadelphia and additional units are now being installed to meet the overwhelming demand for the CROWNTAINER.

CROWN CORK & SEAL COMPANY
Beverage Can Division
BALTIMORE, MD.

Two More Brewing Companies Adopt Crown Cork & Seal Beer Cans

The Fehr Brewing Company of Louisville, Kentucky, is located in one of the oldest horse racing sections in the United States, a fact which they readily capitalized on. Entering the can package field for the first time they desired a package which would be attention getting and easily recognized. Both problems were solved by having a horse racing scene lithographed in four colors and which extended entirely around the can. This feature makes the package easily recognizable from any position and consumers have developed a habit of asking for the "Horse Race" beer. The cans were designed and manufactured by the Crown Cork & Seal Company.

When the Terre Haute Brewing Co., Inc., of Terre Haute, Ind., advertised their Champagne Velvet Brand as "The Beer with a Million Dollar Flavor," they backed it up with a $1,000,000 flavor protection policy reinsured in fifteen legal reserve insurance companies all in the United States. A facsimile of this policy is lithographed on the side of their new twelve-ounce can which they have had on the market since the last week in June. These cans also were manufactured by Crown Cork & Seal Company.

Brewer's Journal August 1940

The Illinois Brewery of Thornton, Ill., have entered the can package filed with two entries. They package a Pilsener under their own label and an extra pale beer for Frederick Bros. of Chicago. Crown Cork & Seal Co. cans are used for both products.

Brewer's Journal October 1940

IN ALL THE WORLD . . . .
NO OTHER CONTAINER LIKE THIS!

Unique in containers for beer is this dramatically designed, sales-stimulating CROWNTAINER—*made without top or side seam!* ◆ Consumers are struck by the smart, ultra-modern appearance of this new container which won an award in the All-America Package Competition. They also like its easy-to-handle shape. ◆ The CROWNTAINER is actually a bottle of *steel*, protected by an aluminum coating, which impressively lends itself to eye-catching decoration in color. ◆ Because of its smooth, Fermax-coated interior, every particle of the original vat-brewed body and flavor of the beer is fully retained. ◆ The CROWNTAINER goes through filling and capping machinery like a *bottle*—and the smooth, tapering shoulder facilitates *complete* air escape when filling. ◆ Your nearest CCS Representative will gladly furnish you with complete information, samples and prices.

CROWN CORK & SEAL CO.
Beverage Can Division
BALTIMORE, MARYLAND

THE CROWNTAINER

Crown 12 oz. and quart size cans are as fine as any you can buy. With them goes an unmatched service to help you adapt your bottling lines quickly, easily and at the lowest possible cost.

CROWNTAINER –

The Ultra-Modern Container for Beer –

Package-minded brewers are finding the new Crowntainer much to their liking. Introduced just a short time ago, the demand is already overwhelming.

This ultra modern container is made without top seam or side seam. It is literally a steel bottle, protected by an aluminum coating, and readily lends itself to beautiful decoration in color. With its smooth shoulders and sides, it presents a striking appearance and has many important advantages.

In Crowntainer, CCS has pioneered an entirely new container for beer— different in appearance and different in construction. For complete information, call the CCS Representative.

CROWN CORK AND SEAL CO.
Beverage Can Division
BALTIMORE, MARYLAND

Crown 12 oz. and quart size cans are as fine as any you can buy. With them goes an unmatched service to help you adapt your bottling lines quickly, easily and at lowest cost.

CCS CANS
are beer!

THERE is a real surprise for the brewing industry in the new CCS Cans for beer. They have definite improvements and advantages, never before available.

DISTINCTIVE APPEARANCE. At the first glance you see that CCS Cans are different. Taller, slimmer and well proportioned, they have a distinctive appearance and one that is most attractive.

IMPROVED CONSTRUCTION. More important are the improvements in their construction and manufacture. CCS Cans are made from cold rolled steel . . . a denser, stronger metal and a new departure in beer cans. Although the metal is stronger, CCS Cans actually weigh less.

EXCLUSIVE CCS LINING. A feature of vital interest to every brewer is the new and exclusive CCS Lining. Developed in the CCS Laboratories, with full benefit of this company's long experience in the brewing industry, it maintains the cleanliness, flavor and appearance of beer.

LITHOGRAPHED OR PLAIN. CCS Cans are available either lithographed in colors or plain, as desired. This is a feature which many brewers will find pleasing since plain cans with paper labels offer a definite saving in cost. Paper labels, when attached with waterproof glue, are handsome and serviceable. Their use assures quicker service on can deliveries and far greater flexibility for brewers who market several products or brands.

For complete information on CCS Cans, write, wire or phone your nearest CCS Office.

CROWN CORK AND SEAL COMPANY
CAN DIVISION

BALTIMORE, MD. • PHILADELPHIA, PA. (ACME CAN CO.)

FLAT TOP CANS   ★   CROWN TOP CANS

Brewer's Journal September 1936

FOR PACKAGE-MINDED BREWERS

Brewers everywhere are acclaiming this ultra-modern container for beer. It's different in construction ... different in appearance ... and "tops" in consumer appeal.

Made without top seam or side seam, the CROWNTAINER is streamlined for utility as well as appearance. There are no protrusions to catch foreign matter or water. The smooth, tapering shoulder facilitates complete air escape when filling. And the smooth interior, coated with Fermax, gives lasting protection for the beer.

Get the "inside story" on this new sales producing package. Call the CCS Representative for full information.

CROWN CORK & SEAL COMPANY
Beverage Can Division
BALTIMORE, MD.

PREMIUM PACKAGE RECENTLY ADOPTED BY
WACKER BREWING COMPANY
LANCASTER, PA.

THE CROWNTAINER

Crown 12 oz. and quart size cans are as fine as any you can buy. With them goes an unmatched service to help you adapt your bottling lines quickly, easily and at lowest cost.

Brewer's Journal October 1940

ANOTHER FAMOUS NAME APPEARING ON THE

CROWNTAINER

In the short time that the CROWNTAINER has been available to brewers, many famous names have appeared on its smooth, seamless sides. The industry has received this distinctive container with great enthusiasm. It is different in appearance ... different in construction ... *modern,* appealing and practical.

Built without top seam or side seam, the CROWNTAINER is actually a steel bottle, coated with a protective film of aluminum. Its smooth sides and shoulders lend to its ease of decoration ... and consumers welcome its smart lines and easy-to-pour construction. For information, call the CCS Representative.

CROWN CORK AND SEAL COMPANY
Beverage Can Division
BALTIMORE, MARYLAND

Crown 12 oz. and quart size cans are as fine as any you can buy. With them goes an unmatched service to help you adapt your bottling lines quickly, easily and at lowest cost.

Brewer's Journal June 1940

Quart Cans BY CROWN

THE NEW CROWNTAINER

C. Schmidt & Sons Inc. of Philadelphia is one of the first to adopt the CROWNTAINER—the unique steel bottle for beer recently introduced by CROWN.

The demand for beer in quart size cans is increasing. Why not get YOUR share of this profitable business?

Quart Cans by CROWN are produced under Crown's high standards. They meet every test as a quality container. And CCS Engineers can show you how to adapt your bottling lines . . . quickly, easily and at lowest cost.

Take advantage of the unmatched service that Crown offers in installing cans. Write today for prices and complete information.

CROWN CORK AND SEAL COMPANY CCS

BEVERAGE CAN DIVISION . . . . . BALTIMORE, MARYLAND

Misc. Articles

82

Canned Beer Makes Start in England

JUST A FEW MONTHS AGO AN observer from England made an investigation of the packaging of beer in cans in the United States, and his report was an adverse one as to the practicability of canned beer in England. However, through the activity of the Metal Box Company, Limited, of London, England, beer in cans has made considerable headway during recent months. Realizing that both the antis and the pros in this country will be interested in this development, we asked the manufacturers of the English can to give us a statement. They very obligingly did so through H. K. S. Lindsay of the company's development Department. His statement follows:

"Relating to the beer cans produced by this company, I am enclosing a copy of the brochure which we have prepared for the brewers on this subject; also a brief report of the situation in this country, which includes the advantages which we claim for the consumer and the brewer.

"Our can is made of lithographed tinplate, which is lacquered on the inside and coated with a special wax which is sprayed on the inside of the tin after the latter is made up.

"You will observe that the cone top of the English tin is deeper than that on its American counterpart. This is to facilitate opening of the can by the standard English crown cork opener, which will not open American cans.

"You will observe, also, that we have been able to dispense with the ribs in the cones. The capacity of the standard tins used in this country is one-half of an Imperial pint: 12 oz. tins are made for export. The only canned beer sold in this country is in cans of our manufacture."

Following is a copy of the Brochure referred to:

Brief Facts About Canned Beer

As in the case of canned foods, the idea originated in the United States. Commencing last year, the output there has now reached four million cans of beer per day.

The Metal Box Company Limited are now introducing a similar container in this country. They have found it necessary to improve the interior coating, in order to meet the more critical demands of the British brewer and the British public.

More than eighty leading brewers in Great Britain are experimenting with canned beer and reports received indicate a real measure of success. It is anticipated that within the next few months it will be on sale in most parts of the country. At the moment, four breweries are actually canning and nine others have definitely placed orders for cans. It is anticipated that many more will do so in the near future.

It is not, however, expected that the can will replace the bottle: it will definitely open up new markets for the brewer at home and abroad, and it should consequently increase the consumption of beer.

The following advantages are claimed for beer in cans:

The Consumer

(1) The obvious advantages of the can for use at picnics, hiking, sporting events, yachting, etc. Lighter and takes up less space than bottles, and does not break.
(2) No deposit required on cans; hygienic, used only once.
(3) Cans of beer, compact and light, slip easily into the pocket. They avoid the prejudice of a large section of the public to carrying a bottle.
(4) The can does not admit light— it is acknowledged that light has an unfavorable effect on beer.

The Brewer

(1) Losses through breakages are entirely eliminated.
(2) Storage space is reduced. Cans occupy 60 per cent of the space required by bottles and no space is necessary for returned empties. Capital value of bottle stock eliminated.
(3) The processes of bottle washing and labelling are eliminat d. Cans ready for filling are dev-

It's arrived!

SAVES SPACE - NO BREAKAGES

BEER

CREATES NEW MARKETS

Full details from

THE METAL BOX COMPANY LTD.

QUEEN'S HOUSE, KINGSWAY, LONDON, W.C.2

ELEVEN BREWERIES
HAVE NOW ORDERED
BEER CANS

ered to the brewers in hygienic containers already lithographed to any required design.

(4) Cans can be conveyed from point to point with greater safety and celerity than bottles, and at less cost.

(5) Shorter time is required for pasteurization.

(6) Bookkeeping on returns is eliminated, as cans are not returnable and checking up of deposits and returns automatically disappears.

(7) Transport costs are reduced. A case of canned beer weighs less than half that of bottled beer, and occupies but 60 per cent of the space.

(8) Freight and insurance charges on the glass are so high in the case of bottled beer that its export is limited. Unbreakable cans open up for the brewer an export market which was previously non-existent.

(9) Opens up new markets at home as well as abroad. The brewer stands to reap very considerable new trade if only a small percentage of those who take a drink in their public houses acquire the habit of slipping a can into their pockets.

Schaefer Sets New Note in Beer Can Design

BEER IN CANS IS STILL A new idea. With few exceptions, beer can designs were born in a rush and have been very commercial. Because of cost, colors, in most cases, have been limited to four. Two essentials have not been kept in mind: good taste in use and good shelf display.

The new Schaefer beer can, therefore, strikes a new note in that it meets with the following requirements:

1. Its general appearance of a small wooden keg indicates quality, character, and gives the impression of substance. The package is good from a design standpoint and fits on the table along with the fine linen and silver.

2. The package meets the requirement of the dealer in good shelf display and good stacking value.

3. The red and black label on the can is similar to the label appearing on the bottled beer, thereby maintaining the family resemblance.

While Schaefer beer in cans is just being introduced to the trade, salesmen, retailers and wholesalers are most enthusiastic in their reception of the package and predict it will be a big factor in its sale to the consumer.

To secure display space for packaged beer in groceries and other outlets, the Trommer Breweries of Brooklyn, N. Y., and Orange, N. J., designed an "On Ice" floor stand in colors, as shown above.

Brewer's Journal September 1940

Brewer's Journal October 1936

Bottles and Cans

Developments are coming fast in the matter of Canned Beer—also as to the adoption of the Non-Returnable Bottle, which is now being offered by several bottle companies. The Joseph Schlitz Brewing Company is the latest of the large breweries to adopt cans, they having chosen the Continental. Some of the smaller breweries have also told us of their intention to "try the cans." Several breweries, among them some of the best known, are offering the "Stubby" bottle to their trade.

As we have said before, we don't pretend to know what percentage of bottles or cans will be used one year, two or five years hence. Nobody can possibly know. After all, the public will decide the issue. In the meantime brewers should, as we have said before, study this subject from the peculiarities of their own trade—and act accordingly.

There is, however, one very important thought we would like to pass on to the industry, and it is this: If the brewing industry, in general accord, would advertise and merchandise BEER in the same degree as Canned Beer has been advertised and merchandised, there would be such an increased demand for beer that the can companies, the bottle companies —yes—even the barrel manufacturers—would find themselves so "loaded" with business that we would have a regular "ring-around-the-rosie" jubilee! That is something for the brewers as well as the bottle, keg and can manufacturers to give a lot of serious thought to.

In the meantime, as the Cincinnati Enquirer said editorially, during the week of the Master Brewers' Convention:

"Fortunately, this battle of bottle and can is going to be

Piel Bros. of Brooklyn Advertise the "Stubby" Bottle

fought out peacefully. Verbal bullets and the bombing raids of advertising campaigns will settle the issue without resort to brute violence between the protagonists. And in the long run the consumers of beer will be the arbiters. Although they do not cast ballots, they will buy as they see fit. And under the laws of competition, the bottle or can purveyors will have to accept the arbitrament as gracefully as they are able."

Northampton (Pa.) Brewing Co. Puts Out Beer in National Cans

An American Can Beer Ad

How the Continentl Can Advertises

90

Coors Offers Customers Choice of "Cans" or "Stubbies"

by Lucius S. Flint

Adolph Coors, Golden, Colo.

THAT IT PAYS TO GIVE the customer a choice in modernized packages has been proved in an interesting way by the Adolph Coors Co., Golden, Colo.

In the latter part of November, this Colorado brewery introduced the new type, stubby bottles. About the middle of December cans were added to the packaging list. In December, business increased about 100 per cent. In January, it picked up nearly 50 per cent. The new packages are believed to have been at least partially responsible for these remarkable gains.

Whereas many brewers have limited themselves to one or the other of the new packages, Coors has felt that both are needed to give really complete service. Sales figures indicate that cans are needed in the shipping territory much more than in the local market. In Denver, bottles run four to one against cans, while in California and other distant markets, about 90 per cent of the business is done in cans.

Both packages are available in the territory as well as at Denver. It's just a case of demand. Local people know the beer and know that they are getting a quality product, regardless of what type of container it comes in. Distant customers feel that the brew is more likely to get to them in its original first-class condition when in a sealed container.

The price differential, of course, varies somewhat in different territories. In Denver, the canned product costs five cents extra on individual unit sales or 40 cents per case extra.

The first step in introducing the new packages was to gradually bring in as many as possible of the distributors. They were shown through the company's remodeled plant, shown the new bottles, told of their advantages and given detailed information on how to put them across. As fast as possible distributors from even the most distant states are being brought in for personal conferences and to visit the plant.

Experience has proved to this firm that neither the most elaborate bulletins nor visits of brewery representatives to the distributor territories have the same effect as plant inspections and conferences with officials. When a distributor is seen where and how the brew he sells is produced and is personally acquainted with its manufacturers, he has a lot more to sell than otherwise. He himself is more sold on the product than ever before.

Advertising

The Coors Company has taken full advantage of its new packages from an advertising standpoint. The new bottle was introduced to the public through a full page newspaper advertisement in two colors, red and black. In the illustration of the bottle, they were blended so as to give the impression of a third shade —that of the beer bottle.

A striking headline layout was (Continued on page 92)

The Flavor Hit of the Year

Coors GOLDEN

Export Lager

Double Aged

in **Cans** and Stubby Bottles

It is fitting that Coors Export Lager, *America's finest beer,* should come to you in your choice of two re-styled containers... the compact stubby bottle ... the Keglined Golden Can. Coors Export Lager is a true Vienna type beer processed especially for particular people from the rarest and most costly ingredients in crystal clear Rocky Mountain Spring water. Then, too, this golden brew is *double-aged* to produce a velvet-smooth, mellow-rich flavor not found in any other beer on this continent. Be particular. . . . Specify. Say Coors, *of course,* next time you're dry.

Coors GOLDEN Export Lager BEER

Coors Golden Keglined Cans

Coors GOLDEN Export Lager BEER

A Product of ADOLPH COORS COMPANY, GOLDEN, COLORADO

Type of Newspaper Ad Used by Coors

Coors Advertising
(Continued from page 90.)
obtained. The top headline, in black, read, "Advent of a Million Dollar Flavor." Then, in white, on a black circle appeared: "Coors Golden." The next headline, also in white, was set against a ribbon of red. The wording was: "Export Lager." And finally, the first two words in black and the last in white, all on another red strip, came: "Double Aged Beer." The complete headline: "Advent of a Million Dollar Flavor, Coors Golden Export Lager, Double Aged Beer."

A unique feature of illustration of the new bottle was its comparison with the new size. At the left was shown the new package—in color. To the right was a shadowy outline of the old, tall bottle. Between the two was a ruler, showing the new height as only a little over six and one-half inches, as compared with the old height of more than nine and one-half. A banner line across the right hand illustration—in red against white—read: "Holds as much as tall bottle."

Copy on the new container read: " 'Stubby' is America's newest beer bottle—a new, modern, compact and convenient de-

sign which takes practically as little room in the ice box as a can and holds as much as the old-style, tall bottles. Its rich, brown color shields the contents from light and its graceful curves add attractiveness to table settings, brick bars and counters. You'll like 'Stubby' and you'll like the Coors Golden Export Beer that comes in it. Order a case of Coors new 'Stubbies' today."

The balance of the ad was devoted to illustrations of the remodeled plant and a description of the quality of the new product and its methods of production.
(Continued on page 93.)

TROMMER'S "STUBBY" WINS FIRST PRIZE
For the first time since the All-America Package Competition was instituted four years ago, a beer bottle was awarded top honor, the Gold Award for 1935. Trommer's White Label beer in the "Stubby" bottle, brewed by John F. Trommer, Inc., Brooklyn, N. Y., was the choice of the judges for the most attractive package in the glass bottle and jar division. The "Stubby" bottle used by the Trommer brewery is manufactured by Owens-Illinois Glass Company of Toledo, Ohio. The contest is sponsored by "Modern Packaging" and the prize, a gold figurine, emblematic of merit, was awarded to the Trommer Company at the All-America dinner held in the Hotel Pennsylvania on March 4. This dinner was attended by more than 300 manufacturers of package products.

Trommer's White Label beer is an all-malt brew of premium quality that has been successfully sold by the Trommer organization for many years. George F. Trommer is president of the company and William A. Strassel sales manager of the bottling department.

BALLANTINE RECEIVES PACKAGING AWARD
Leading the way in last summer's preliminary bout between the can and the bottle for America's favorite drink, the already famous triple-circle trademark of Ballantine's beer can added to its laurels by its selection for the Gold Award in its class at the All-America Package Competition in which nearly 10,000 packages were judged in the selection of 41 winners. Opinions may be divided on the new tin packaging for beer, but Ballantine's striking package certainly sets a pace for design, color treatment, consumer service, and saving, that fully justifies the attention it has received. The cans used by Ballantine are made by the American Can Co.

93

Coors Advertising

(Continued from page 92)

Following the introductory ad on the new bottles came a series of smaller newspaper advertisements featuring the two containers. Much the same headline layout used in the original ad was employed in the smaller ones.

Here's the copy used on one par-

ticularly effective ad: "It is fitting that Coors Export Lager, America's finest beer, should come to you in your choice of two re-styled containers . . . the compact, stubby bottle . . . the Keglined Golden Can." The rest of the paragraph was concerned with the beer itself.

In Denver, the firm has been running four column by 12 inch ads twice a week, while in the state and in three California cities, a three

column by nine inch size has been used at the same rate of frequency.

Gradually, the two new types of containers are being subordinated to other appeals, but, the two illustrations will be carried as a regular feature and brief copy will be used for some time. One appeal being used is that beer is not only more refreshing than cocktails, but also leaves a person feeling better afterward.

Brewer's Journal March 1936

Two New Tools for Opening Canned Beer

SPOUTER and POR EZY are two new openers for canner beer. They are new additions to our regular line of Spouter openers for opening cans containing all kinds of liquids.

POR EZY is a better steel opener for both canned and bottled beer. It opens all kinds of cans containing fruit and vegetable juices. It cuts a nicer opening which permits easy pouring and emptying of the can. Por Ezy openers are made from selected steel, carefully heat treated and hardened. They are

finished in lacquered gun-metal, or bright nickel.

The new Spouter press type opener for counter or serving tables is lever operated. A downward pressure of this lever opens the cans and forms a nice pouring spout. It is the ideal fixture for all up-to-date places where canned beer is served. Finished in white glazed porcelain, also lacquer finish. The bottoms of these openers are covered with felt to prevent scratching furniture and each opener is individually boxed.

Both of these products are protected by patents issued December 24, 1935, granted to Air Scale Company, Toledo Ohio, the manufacturers.

Showing New Tools for Opening Canned Beer

Brewer's Journal May 1936

by Richard J. La Susa #609 et al

❖❖

[*The editor wishes to thank Pat Jones of the United States Brewers Association for cooperation in making the* Brewers Journal *advertisement reprints available.*]

BCCA

No one ever dreamed it would grow so fast, but the Beer Can Collectors of America represented an idea whose time had come. The seed was planted in October, 1969, when the St. Louis *Globe-Democrat* ran a short article on Denver Wright, Jr.'s unique hobby—beer can collecting. Five other St. Louis area citizens read it with special interest, because they, too, collected beer cans. They were amazed to find someone else with the same hobby, let alone someone who was willing to talk openly about it.

The six men—Denver, Tony Bruning, Bob Eckert, Ken Fanger, Ray White, and Denver's brother Larry—soon began meeting socially to talk beer cans and to view each other's collections. If one had extra cans he didn't need for his own collection, he'd bring them to one of the meetings and give them to the other men. This was the beginning of BCCA's primary activity—beer can trading.

I never
saw a can
I didn't like!

After several meetings, Larry Wright suggested they form a club in hopes of finding still more people interested in can collecting. As Bob Eckert later put it, "We knew someday there would be a club for this hobby, so we figured we might as well be the ones to start it." Accordingly, the Beer Can Collectors of America (BCCA) was born on April 15, 1970, complete with a constitution and by-laws. Officers were Denver Wright, president; Larry Wright, vice-president; Bob Eckert, secretary; and Ken Fanger, treasurer. Larry and Bob later went on to become presidents of the organization.

Each founding member agreed their new club should be strictly a "fun" group, promoting the collection, trading and display of beer cans. Membership was open to everybody, regardless of age, sex, race, or income. They were to build their collections by trading with other members—helping somebody else while they helped themselves. By the end of the year, the fledgling group counted 30 members from 14 states and Canada.

DON'T KICK THE CAN!

BCCA never needed a high-powered membership drive, for most new members were finding it. Many saw newspaper articles about current members, while word of mouth brought the message to others. By September, 1971, the club boasted 304 members from 35 states and Canada. It was about this time that BCCA started assigning membership numbers, giving each member a number indicating the order in which he had joined.

When BCCA was formed, no member had a particularly large collection—Bob Eckert's was tops at 608 cans—but each man had several cans that none of the others had. Somebody soon wondered how many different cans had ever been produced. Although the collectors knew they'd probably never find the answer, they decided to try.

BEER CANS DON'T LITTER... PEOPLE DO!

Each charter member submitted an inventory of his collection to the club secretary, listing each brand, its brewery, and the brewery's location. The secretary tabulated the results, which became the first composite list. By the end of 1970, it listed more than 1,200 brands. Each new member had to submit an inventory of his collection upon joining, so by September, 1971, the composite had grown so long that each new member was asked only to submit the names of brands he had that weren't already on the master list. This requirement is still in effect, keeping the composite up-to-date.

Reprinted annually, it now lists some 5,000 different brands, including a separate section for foreign cans. This number doesn't include major label changes and the different labels produced concurrently by a particular brand, such as the 21 different scenes in the Schmidt outdoors series. If the BCCA counted changes and varieties, the composite would probably list 15,000 cans.

In addition to the composite, BCCA also publishes and distributes to members an alphabetical roster, listing each member's name, address, occupation, phone number, birthdate, and spouse's name. Another roster lists members by their membership number and still another geographically. These are an invaluable aid in helping members get acquainted and trade by mail.

Accompanying each name in the roster are a number of stars, indicating how many cans are in the member's collection. These stars, which also appear on the membership certificate, assign each collector a ranking as follows:

  *Brewery Worker (100-249 cans)
  **Apprentice Brewer (250-499 cans)
  ***Journeyman Brewer (500-749 cans)
  ****Brewmaster (750-999 cans)
  *****Grand Brewmaster (1,000 or more cans)

The star systems injects a spirit of friendly competition into BCCA as members strive to attain Grand Brewmaster status—several hundred have made it so far. More than that, however, the star system is a useful trading tool, as a one star member would seldom get too far sending a trading list to a member with 2,000 cans in his collection.

As the new club's membership spread far beyond St. Louis, the need for regular communication grew and in March, 1971, the BCCA *News Report* was established. Beginning as a four-page quarterly fact sheet, the *News Report* has grown to a full-fledged, 40-page, two-color magazine published six times a year. It fosters a sense of belonging to the club while spreading information about beer, cans, breweries, and club members. Larry Wright (#2 in BCCA) edited it from its birth until September, 1975, when Lonnie Smith (#99 in BCCA) of Denver took over the job.

In the summer of 1975 BCCA began monthly publication of their *Want Ad Bulletin* edited by Dave Ohlendorf (#1603).

As the months passed and BCCA grew even more farflung, it sought a way to bring as many members together as possible to get acquainted and enjoy a mammoth trading session. Since businesses and large social or fraternal organizations hold national conventions, it seemed only natural for this new club to have one, too.

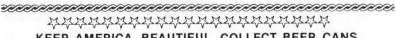

KEEP AMERICA BEAUTIFUL COLLECT BEER CANS

Gambling that response would justify the effort, in 1971 the club's board chose St. Louis as its convention city and the Holiday Inn in suburban Sunset Hills as the convention center. The meet was scheduled for Friday, September 24, through Sunday, September 26.

Where it all began, Canventionwise.

Any fears about low attendance vanished early Friday afternoon as members trekked in from 17 states and Canada, bringing with them an estimated 100,000 cans to trade. Before the weekend was over, attendance totaled 232 members and guests. A formal trading session was slated for Saturday afternoon, but swapping began with the first arrivals and continued through late Sunday. Most members went home with 50 to 100 new cans.

First Convention. Courtyard of the Holiday Inn St. Louis. Saturday afternoon, as people were setting up for trading session.

It was at the St. Louis meet that one of BCCA's more colorful members, Lew Cady (#98) of Denver, proposed that future conventions be called something less conventional. He suggested the word *can*vention, which caught on immediately and has since become a byword among beer can collectors.

In addition to the cans they trade for, members attending a canvention go home with a commemorative can. The cans usually carry BCCA's logo on the front and the year's officers and board members on the back. Commemoratives are rarely traded as each member gets only one.

The St. Louis canvention attracted media coverage like an abandoned brewery does can collectors. The club and its unique gathering appeared on radio and television and in a number of newspapers. Thanks to this coverage, BCCA grew even faster until September, 1972, showed it with 609 members.

When the BCCA toured the Anheuser-Busch plant in St. Louis, Ian Russel (Toronto) and Max Robb (Colorado) really lapped it up. It as their belief that the stream running from the brewery was beer. Others note that the alley was only about 100' from the Clydesdale's barn.

This growth, strongest in the midwestern states, made formation of chapters the next logical step.

The Wisconsin Chapter was the first, beginning operations in early February, 1972. St. Louis' Gateway Chapter followed in the same month and since has become the club's largest with more than 400 members. St. Louis is also home of a unique BCCA subdivision—the McDonnell Douglas Chapter—with membership limited to employees of that corporation.

By 1976 there were 49 chapters in 20 states, Washington, D.C. and the Canal Zone, sporting such beer-inspired names as Olde Frothingslosh, Mile Hi, Simon Pure, KC's Best, Blackhawk, Horlacher, Paul Bunyan and Lone Star. All operate as independent organizations, with membership in the BCCA usually a general membership requirement. Each holds several trading sessions during the year, along with other social functions.

Although it was held at the Playboy Club in Lake Geneva, Wisconsin, attendees paid more attention to *beer* cans than any other kind at BCCA's second canvention in September, 1972. Some 528 members and guests attended, bringing their traders in everything from car trunks to U-Haul trailers. The club's first display contest, in which individual members and chapters vied for prizes by showing off up to 100 of their prize cans, was a highlight.

It was also at Lake Geneva that mortician Armin "Shorty" Hotz (#131), when informed the club boasted another funeral director among its ranks, said "I'd like to get together with him sometime and share a cold one!"

If BCCA had an underexposure problem before Lake Geneva, it didn't afterward. The New York *Times* wrote a feature article on the event and *Modern Brewing Age* magazine covered it. The *Times* article was syndicated to newspapers from coast to coast, plus in Mexico City and Hong Kong. The Canvention also drew extensive radio and television coverage. Adding to the publicity, in November, 1972, *Oui* magazine carried a Lew Cady article on beer can collecting.

As a result, the club's secretary was swamped with membership applications from foam fanatics worldwide. Before 1973 saw its last trading session, BCCA boasted over 1,700 members from 48 states, the District of Columbia, Puerto Rico, the Canal Zone, Canada, England, Sweden, and Japan. The 1973 Canvention was held in Cincinnati; 1974's in Denver; 1975's in Des Moines. The 1976 Canvention will be in Philadelphia; '77 in Kansas City; '78 in Milwaukee.

Although many people joining had never collected cans before, most new members had enjoyed their hobby for years, completely unaware there were possibly thousands of others doing the same thing. Hearing there were so many others usually created an immediate bond of loyalty between the club and the member, lending a sense of dignity to a hobby most people thought required being "some kind of nut".

This sense of belonging was cemented by BCCA decals, window stickers, t-shirts, stationery, and a number of other items all bearing the club's registered logo of a hand reaching for a beer can.

As this book is being published, BCCA is planning to purchase a building in the St. Louis area and establish a Beer Can Museum which also will house the club's national headquarters.

One of BCCA's most ambitious projects was completed in September 1975 when it published its *Guide to United States Beer Cans.* The book contains nearly 3,000 individual photos of beer cans and is an invaluable tool for the collector who trades by mail. The club plans larger editions in the future.

Bob McClure and Frank and Cindy Visconti. As a host for Canvention III, McClure was busy helping people check in.

Glenn Thorsen (#320), President of BCCA Wisconsin Chapter presents 1973 BCCA Can of the Year Trophy to Fred Huber.

Three mile hi chapter members (one of whom is 6' 8'') stand by giant cylinder of empty beer cans constructed following a banquet in Cincinnati.

1974's Miss Beer Can, Debbie Burden of Denver, Colorado

A few of the 1974 Canventioneers at Canvention IV in Denver

More than 1,700 persons attened the 1975 Canvention banquet in Des Moines Veterans Auditorium.

Canvention V's Miss Beer Can, Chris Jennings.

None of BCCA's charter members foresaw its already tremendous growth in five short years. Perhaps the reason is because the hobby offers good, clean, economical fun to everyone, regardless of age, race, sex or income level. It's often a family affair. Much of the credit should go to a few dedicated individuals who have given so much of their time and talent performing the functions necessary to make such a large organization go—and all of it for no pay. Their reward: the success the club has enjoyed and will continue to enjoy.

Where Beer Can Collectors of America will go in the years ahead is anybody's guess. Its growth shows no sign of slowing down—by early 1976 there were nearly 9,000 registered collectors. Each member is still caught up in the fun and enjoyment, and each new can they trade for brings a new friend and only baits their interest in tomorrow.

by Robert Eckert #3 et al

APPENDIX I

PAST OFFICERS OF BCCA

April 1970 - September 1971:
PRESIDENT: Denver Wright, Jr. #1   VICE PRES.: Larry Wright #2
SECRETARY: Robert Eckert #3   TREASURER: Ken Fanger #4

October 1971 - September 1972:
PRESIDENT: Larry Wright #2   VICE PRES.: Robert Eckert #3
SECRETARY: Jerry Glader #57   TREASURER: Gil Brennell #13

October 1972 - September 1973:
PRESIDENT: Robert Eckert #3   VICE PRES.: Jerry Glader #57
                                     (Replaced by
                                     Lou Kovarik #77)
SECRETARY: Henry Herbst #70   TREASURER: Rich VonBehren #113

October 1973 - September 1974:
PRESIDENT: Gil Brennell #13   VICE PRES.: Henry Herbst #70
SECRETARY: Fred Haveland #352   TREASURER: Jerry Weishaar #159

October 1974 - September 1975:
PRESIDENT: Henry Herbst #70   VICE PRES: Jerry Weishaar #159
SECRETARY: Hal Leeker #843   TREASURER: Jim Thole #410

October 1975 - September 1976:
PRESIDENT: Jerry Weishaar #159   VICE PRES.: Hal Leeker #843
SECRETARY: Bob Feldwisch #406   TREASURER: Jim Thole #410

APPENDIX II

VOTED BCCA CAN OF THE YEAR

1972   Fyfe & Drum (Genesee Brewing Co.)
1973   Our Beer (Huber Brewing Co.)
1974   Colorado Gold Label (Walter Brewing Co.)
1975   Acme (Acme Brewing Co.)

VOTED BCCA COLLECTOR OF THE YEAR

1972   Ernie Oest #108, Port Jefferson, N.Y.
1973   Denver Wright, Jr. #1, Frontenac, Mo.
1974   Clayton Tichelar #701, Chicago, Ill.
1975   Larry Wright #2, St. Louis, Mo.

APPENDIX III

CANVENTION I (1971) in St. Louis, Mo., Attending Members 146, Guests 86, Total 232 and States & Countries 17 plus Canada

CANVENTION II (1972) in Lake Geneva, Wisc., Attending Members 283, Guests 245, Total 528 and States & Countries 26 plus Canada.

CANVENTION III (1973) in Cincinnati, Ohio, Attending Members 563, Guests 404, Total 967 and States & Countries 33 plus DC & Canada.

CANVENTION IV (1974) in Denver, Colo., Attending Members 519, Guests 343, Total 862 and States & Countries 34 plus Canada & Canal Zone.

CANVENTION V (1975) in Des Moines, Iowa, Attending Members 1023, Guests 770, Total 1793 and States & Countries 35 plus Canada.

The following members attended each of the first five BCCA Canventions:

BCCA #	NAME	CITY & STATE
1	Denver Wright, Jr.	Frontenac, MO
2	Larry Wright	Saint Louis, MO
9	John Ahrens	Moorestown, NJ
10	Vaughn Amstutz	Lafayette, IN
13	Gil Brennell	Saint Louis, MO
23	Harry Keithline	Saint Louis, MO
24	Delmar Nozicka	Wahoo, NEB.
28	Harold Lorenz	Cedar Falls, IA
33	Bill Christensen	Madison, NJ
41	Rich Behnen	Saint Louis, MO
42	John Paul	Cincinnati, OH
45	Marvin Rowley	Hobart, IN
53	John Soltesz, Jr.	Highland, IN
65	Jack Turner	Florissant, MO
70	Henry Herbst	Shrewsbury, MO
77	Lou Kovarik	Saint Louis, MO
85	Walter Hintz	Hales Corners, WI
98	Lew Cady	Denver, CO
99	Lonnie Smith	Denver, CO
103	Alfred Mallet	Munster, IN
104	Bob McClure	Worthington, OH
116	Max Robb	Central City, CO
119	Robert Leslie	Worthington, OH
131	Armin Hotz	St. Peter, IL
133	Raymond Meyer	Saint Louis, MO
136	James McCoy	Denver, CO
137	Edward Wendell	Ellisville, MO
146	Ben Bright	St. Charles, MO
157	Ron Andracsek	Saint Louis, MO
159	Gerald Weishaar	Hazelwood, MO
162	William Miller	Crestwood, MO
166	Kittridge Hall	Ferguson, MO
173	Pat Kelly Frawley	Vancouver, WA
175	Warren Taylor	Brentwood, MO
186	Henry Reinkensmeyer	Hoyleton, IL
193	Bill Helsley	Harrisburg, PA
200	Roger Johnson	Buffalo Grove, IL
205	Walter Fetzer	Strathmore, NJ
210	Jerry Ouper	Berwyn, IL
212	Paul Udvare	Milwaukee, WI
213	Don Villers	Belle Plaine, IA
230	Dan Heiderscheit	Cedar Rapids, IA
232	Curt Fisher	Cedar Rapids, IA
233	Bill Demory	Cedar Rapids, IA
238	Joe Geist	Saint Louis, MO
248	Bruce Gregg	Kansas City, MO
264	F.H. Schwarzbach	Crestwood, MO
266	George Studt	Saint Louis, MO
276	Michael Hillebrand	Eagle Pass, TX
296	Bob Smiley	Cedar Rapids, IA

APPENDIX IV
CHAPTERS OF THE BEER CAN COLLECTORS OF AMERICA
(As of January 1, 1976)

Chapter and state location	Date Founded
Badger Bunch (WI)	2-8-72
Baltimore (MD)	2-16-74
Big Beer Brotherhood (*)	5-1-75
Big Ditch (Canal Zone)	4-25-75
Blackhawk (IL)	9-1-73
Blue Room (IL)	11-12-72
Buckeye (OH)	1-8-74
Bullfrog (IL)	6-6-75
Capitol City (D.C.)	7-16-72
Congress (NY)	7-18-75
Cowboy (WY)	9-1-73
49er's (CA)	5-11-74
Gambrinus (OH)	1-27-74
Garden State (NJ)	4-1-75
Gateway (MO)	2-18-72
Genesse Valley (NY)	11-1-74
Golden State (CA)	6-24-73
Greater Delaware (PA)	11-19-73
Heart of Illinois (IL)	8-1-73
Horlacher (PA)	10-1-73
Johnny Appleseed (OH)	6-5-75
KC Best (MO)	4-21-74
Keystone (PA)	11-9-75
Lakeshore (WI)	1-1-75
Lincoln Land (IL)	10-13-74
Lone Star (TX)	3-13-73
Mardi Gras (LA)	12-3-74
McDonnell Douglas (MO)	8-1-72
Miami Valley (OH)	6-1-73
Michiana (MI)	11-13-75
Mid South (TN)	11-16-73
Mile Hi (CO)	4-12-72
Mizzou Stags (MO)	5-1-73
North Star (MN)	4-8-73
Olde Frothingslosh (PA)	3-1-73
Pioneer City (OH)	11-4-73
Queen City (OH)	11-1-74
Rainer (WA)	3-1-74
Rock River Valley (IL)	1-20-74
Royal Order of the Can Clans (*)	11-20-75
Simon Pure (NY)	11-24-73
Southeast (GA)	8-25-75
Southern Select Group (TX)	7-1-75
Southern Tier (NY)	5-1-75
Star Model (IL)	11-15-75
Star-Peerless (IL)	6-3-75
Strohs Fire Brewed (MI)	11-1-73
Sunshine (FL)	5-6-73
Three Rivers (IN)	4-29-74
Windy City (IL)	6-1-73
Yankee (NY)	10-12-75

*At large

The Only Nut in the World???

A man boards your homeward flight at Dulles International and walks down the aisle with a large rectangular package under his arm. He sits down beside you and as he shoves the package under the seat, you hear an ominous metal clank. You glance apprehensively at your fellow passenger, but he looks away quickly.

One Saturday morning just after you've returned from a Canadian vacation, you wake up to the clatter of garbage can lids in your backyard. Looking out the window, you see a collection of spider bikes in the alley. Their young owners are busy going through your trash.

At the Illinois State Fair in Springfield, you and your family are admiring the Holsteins in one of the dairy barns when a load of refuse from the ages falls on your head. A young man in city clothes looks down at you sheepishly from the attic and apologizes.

These people are not criminals, nor are they pranksters bent on doing malicious mischief at your expense. Strange they are, but that's only because they're beer can hobbyists engaged in the never ending pursuit of more cans. The man on the plane is a businessman returning with a case of empties. The kids are hoping you brought back some beer from your vacation. And the man in the attic has heard that farmers, when the day's judging is over and the cattle are milked and fed, have been known to enjoy a few beers. Rather than clutter up the floor with them, the farmers have for years tossed the empties into the attic. If you look at the refuse which landed on your head, you might spy an Edelweiss cone top. Chances are the man in the attic has found several.

Although it's a wonder such seemingly questionable activities haven't landed more BCCA members in jail, most collectors are less conspicuous. Your next door neighbor might have a hundred cans on display in his den. If he doesn't, then your mailman probably does. Or maybe it's your doctor, lawyer, or neighborhood policeman. If you're a student, your teacher might be a collector. And if you're a teacher, then several of your students probably are.

Although nearly 9,000 people worldwide belong to the club, it's estimated there are thousands of other can collectors.

Most members are male, although an increasing number of women are joining. A few are wives of members, but most are school-teachers, secretaries, accountants, businesswomen, bank clerks or students drawn to the hobby by the same mysterious appeal that attracts their male counterparts.

BCCA members range in age from six to 102. Although nearly half are in their 20's or 30's, roughly 25 percent are younger than that. Not surprisingly, more than a few members don't even drink what's in the containers they so avidly collect.

Many of BCCA's members are teenagers or younger. Some people frown on children collecting cans that once carried an alcoholic beverage. However, as this letter from a young member's mother shows, many parents encourage the hobby.

Dear BCCA Members:

Just thought I'd write and give you a mother's point of view on collecting beer cans. I am very proud of my two teenage sons and their collections. Collecting cans is the best thing that ever happened to them. They spend every free minute either looking for cans, cleaning them, or trading. Almost every night after school we head for a different dump or investigate any possible place that has cans.

At first, I'll admit, I wasn't very happy about finding old rusty cans in the bathroom sink, but now I can't wait till the rust is cleaned off to see the "Big Find". Collecting cans is certainly a family affair involving mothers, fathers, grandmas, aunts, and uncles.

So please tell any mothers that may inquire about teenage sons collecting beer cans the following very true statements:

1. They will become so involved in finding beer cans they won't have time to think about drinking any beer.
2. Your family will certainly be a lot closer.
3. There is no "Generation Gap" in collecting beer cans. . .

Sincerely,

Mrs. Brenda Marron, Mother of Scott (#3294) and Tim Rohrer (future member) Danville, IL.

You can't go to a state in the union without finding a BCCA member. You'll also find them in many foreign countries, particularly Sweden. For a living, members do everything from delivering newspapers to acting or operating their own businesses. Many are retired.

So, BCCA members are like most other Americans. There's no sure way to tell them from the general populace — that is, until you set a beer can down in front of them. Then, well, strange things happen. For example:

Harold "Lefty" Lorenz #28
Cedar Falls, Iowa

It's not hard to pick Lefty Lorenz out of a crowd. He's the Iowa State Trooper driving around town with a row of beer cans on each side of his pickup truck under the sign claiming "Beer Cans Are Beautiful."

A trooper for 28 years, Lefty started collecting while on a trip to Los Angeles in 1965, coming home with such obscure regional brands as Eastside Lager, Eastside Old Tap, Mile Hi, and Tivoli.

The trooper once found 135 cans in an old railroad depot, but that takes a back seat to the time he walked into an abandoned house and found nearly 10,000 old cans. Nearly all of them were *Hamm's* cans from the early 50's, though. Needless to say, Lefty has quite a supply of them and is still ready for trading.

In 1972, Lefty converted his garage into a family room, adding a fireplace with a raised hearth. For posterity's sake, he sealed 50 beer cans in the space between the hearth and the floor. Since then, he has forgotten what he stored away and has cast quite a few longing glances at the hearth, wondering what good traders might be underneath it.

Ernie Oest #108
Port Jefferson, New York

Uncle Ernie may well have been the world's first beer can collector.
He started collecting beer-related items in the 1920's as a schoolboy.
The Dutch style shelving in taverns went out of fashion in that
decade, and as tavern owners tore it down, they often threw away the
steins they had kept on it. It was a simple matter for Ernie to pick a
few up on the way home from school. By the time Prohibition ended,
Ernie had quite a collection of steins, bottles, and signs. When cans
came on the market just two years later, it was only natural that he
should start keeping them, too.

Uncle Ernie had been a machinist for 24 years in 1966 when he quit
to go into the beverage distribution business. He soon moved his by
then enormous collection to his new business, but space there was
limited. Before long, he began planning a museum where he could
display all his breweriana for public enjoyment.

With that in mind, Ernie sold his beverage business and purchased
a 4,000 square foot building in Port Jefferson at 1530 Main Street.
The city fathers wouldn't let him call it a museum, so he named it
"Memories of Beer and Brewing" and moved his collection in. It's
now open from 9 a.m. to 5 p.m. daily and features a snack bar for
hungry travelers.

In recognition of his accomplishments, Ernie Oest was named the
first BCCA Collector of the Year by the club's membership in 1972.

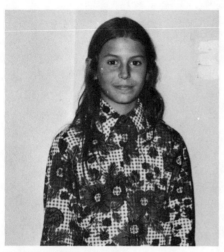

Pam Woodman #1993
Olmsted, Ohio

Pam is the younger half of perhaps BCCA's only father-daughter team. Her father, Leo, has number 868.

Pam is 14 years old and a ninth grader. She needed little help from her father to take up the hobby and saved her pennies, nickels, and dimes until she could pay her own initiation fee and dues.

Pam reports she often gets the "evil eye" from grocery clerks because the first place she heads to when she enters a grocery store is the beer cooler. But stares don't bother her a bit because "people just don't know."

Frank Westhoff #1329
Decatur, Illinois

When you walk into the basement of a Roman Catholic priest's residence and see 5,000 beer cans stored away for trading, you know the hobby has taken hold. Father Frank Westhoff, who has travelled over 75,000 miles to bring runaways back home, had been picking up beer cans for a member of his parish in Springfield, Illinois, for several years when he decided to start a collection of his own in 1973. He already has 900 different cans in addition to his huge trading stock.

Father Westhoff is currently the assistant pastor at St. James Catholic Church in Decatur. He also works in a number of human rights organizations, has promoted the establishment of a new Illinois facility for the retarded, and has played a key role in finding jobs for many probationers and parolees. He teaches, guest lectures at area universities, writes articles for a number of publications, and appears on radio and television on behalf of many causes.

John Ahrens #9
Moorestown, New Jersey

When John was a senior at Yale in 1964, he joined a group of friends who were competing against some other friends to see which one could come up with the most different beer cans. John doesn't say whether his group won or not, but he's been hooked on the hobby ever since. His collection now stands at 9,000 cans. As a college textbook salesman, he has traveled to 20 states, adding to that number all the time.

When John moved from Ohio recently, his beer cans weighed almost 500 pounds. Since they were so bulky, the movers loaded them on the truck first. It was only after everything else was packed in that the movers discovered John's collection didn't put enough weight on the rear wheels of the cab. They had to redistribute the entire load.

Ken Hiestand #218
Lois Hiestand #288
York, Pennsylvania

Although most collectors' wives help them out in their hobby, Lois Hiestand was the first woman to actually join BCCA after her husband had. She was also the first woman to serve on the BCCA board of directors.

The Hiestands started collecting in 1967 on a vacation trip to New England. They now have more than 2,000 cans in their joint collection.

Ann Semple #828
Midland, Texas

Single girls like Ann aren't an oddity in America, but they are in
BCCA. A fourth grade teacher at Emuson Elementary School in
Midland, her collection began in 1970 when a soldier friend brought
her a can from each place he had been stationed. Although she isn't
an active trader, Ann has since added more than 200 cans to her
collection.

Donald Sperr #467
St. Paul, Minnesota

Don, a brewer for 29 years at the Theodore Hamm Company in St. Paul, Minnesota, has been collecting beer cans for 15 years.

"When I saw the first can come off the line 29 years ago, I never dreamed that some day collecting cans would become my hobby," said Don. He presently has about 2,300 cans in his collection.

Don's wife, Donna, and six children often help search for cans.

"My son Dave, 12, takes quite an interest with me in can collecting," said Don. "But when we go looking through solid waste disposal areas in northern Minnesota, the whole family joins in."

These disposal areas are "choice areas" to find beer cans says Don. "The family once spent an entire Easter Sunday in one of these waste areas," he added. "But we had to quit when we dug so deep we hit frost."

William B. Christensen, #33
Madison, New Jersey

Back in 1954 a beer can collector was born. Bill Christensen got the idea from the older brother of one of his friends.

Bill wrote BCCA in 1971, "Your club is certainly a great step forward. Thus far we have all been collecting more or less in the dark, but now with trading and information perhaps the hobby will really catch on."

In 1974 he wrote, "I'm both optimistic and pessimistic. It's great to see more and more people 'seeing the light' with regards to beer can collecting, but I'd hate to see the spirit of informal camraderie which our organization has fostered go by the board with all this growth. We're still fortunate in being a noncommercial avocation where the size or quality of one's collection isn't determined by one's income, but I'm afraid these days may be numbered . . . we'll all still trade cans of course, but I'm afraid we're in a kind of a never, never land as far as commercialism is concerned. Time will tell!"

A professional numismatist, single, a Phi Betta Kappa, member of dozens of numismatist organizations throughout the world, Bill manages to keep busy.

His current inventory of different cans is over the 4,000 mark; 800 of his favorite cans are displayed on shelves, largely New Jersey cans and others that strike his fancy for one reason or the other.

Bud Hack #254
Hartford, Connecticut

While most other collectors talk on and on of someday making a great "find", Bud is happily boasting of the greatest find of his beer can collecting in the person of his lovely wife, Susanne. As the result of his can collecting Bud met and married his wife.

Susanne and Bud came to know each other through her father, Milton "Uncle Milty" Rewer #388. They first met at the Second BCCA Canvention at Lake Geneva, Wisconsin, but it wasn't until a year later in Cincinnati at Canvention III that they realized that they had more going for them than just beer cans. Being the daughter of a collector, Susanne encourages Bud's hobby and participates in can hunting and the fellowship sessions that go along with it.

Bud's collecting began as a lark when he needed six cans to make a mobile. The idea didn't work but the cans were so attractive that he kept them and continued adding to the collection. This was back in 1969 but Bud didn't join BCCA until September, 1971. At the time he had a "big" collection of 124 cans. As of January 1976 he has 2,800 cans in his collection. He prefers to collect only 12 ounce cans except for the foreign cans that come in odd sizes. The cans must be in mint or near perfect condition. He admits this is probably a throwback to his years of stamp and coin collecting where condition is of prime importance. Since Bud is a dealer in stamps and coins (for the past 17 years), he realizes this all the more.

Dick Bjorneby #733
Coco Solo, Canal Zone

Dick started collecting beer cans and bottles about twelve years ago.
A friend of his who was rigger and diver for the Panama Canal noted
one day how many different kinds of foreign beer there seemed to be
on all of the ships that he worked on. This interested Dick and he was
shortly on his way as a can and bottle collector. He collected only
foreign cans and bottles, all full. Today he has about 2,400 cans, and
of course he no longer collects full ones.

Dick is an admeasurer (tonnage surveyor). There are about 32
admeasurers in the Canal Zone and only about 40 in the entire United
States. In his work Dick has boarded more than 800 ships. All
maritime nations have admeasurers who are given the job of
assigning a gross and net tonnage (volume) to each ship under that
nation's flag. Dick admits that between his job as admeasurer, and
as a Panama Canal diver, he has to have had two of the most interesting jobs in the world.

Foreign cans, of course, dominate Dick's 1,400-can collection, a
good part of which he has obtained from surprised ship's captains.

In February 1974, Dick received an award from the Canal Zone
government for his "outstanding voluntary contributions to the Isth-
mian community."

Tom Coury #1164
Clarksdale, Mississippi

While in college at Memphis State University in 1970, Tom was in charge of decorating the recreation room of his fraternity house. He got the idea of taking one can of each brand of beer available in the area and stacking them against the wall behind the bar. At the beginning of this venture there were 23 cans. As each fraternity brother returned from his summer, 1971 vacation he brought Tom a contribution to his efforts. By the time classes resumed in the fall of 1971 the cans had outgrown the allotted space so Tom moved them to his home. He continued adding cans to the collection and in the Spring of 1973 Tom joined the ranks of BCCA. When he made his first trade in July of that year there were 113 cans in the collection. Since then he has traded with more than 600 members and the collection has increased to more than 2,600 cans.

Tom makes his home with his mother. She isn't too interested in Tom's hobby but she does "contribute patience and tolerance".

He is a member of the National Association of Cemeteries, Jaycees, Mensa, and Lambda Chi Aplha Fraternity. He is also president of the Coahoma County Memorial Gardens where he is a cemeterian.

His greatest thrill to date in his beer can collecting adventures came during the 1973 Canvention in Cincinnati when Al Milnar #818 of Gretna, Louisiana, handed him a gift-wrapped package. Tom admits he "went bananas" when he opened the package to find a mint Tiger can by Jackson Brewing Company (no longer in business). This was Tom's local brewery and more than any other can Tom had been wanting a Tiger for a long, long time. He is so proud of this single can that he doesn't dare display it among his other cans. . . . .it has a shelf all to itself!

by Denver Wright, Jr. #1 et al

Finding, Swapping, Showing

Once you've been bitten by the beer can collecting bug, you won't be able to pass a dump, lovers lane, old stage show set, unoccupied building, dilapidated barn, abandoned railroad station, closed brewery, or tavern cellar without at least a cursory search for old beer cans.

The most obvious sources of cans are local package stores and supermarkets. At older liquor stores, ask if there just might be a few older cans from broken six packs tucked away or gathering dust in a back corner. Most beer distributors clear out these cans every few months, but you'll hit pay dirt just often enough to make asking worthwhile.

Next, get to know the beer distributors themselves, particularly the older, well established firms. Some distributors may still have anywhere from a few older cans to dozens of cases of oldies just taking up room in their warehouses.

Friends and relatives, or even perfect strangers, can help build your collection. Many home craftsmen have an old can or two sitting on their workbenches—usually full of nuts and bolts. They'll be only too happy to exchange them for a modern Budweiser can.

Friends can also help you add foreign cans to your collection. Never let anyone leave the country without reminding him that you're a collector and would appreciate a can or two from wherever he's going (six packs come next, then full cases). It's a good idea to tell your friends what brands are canned in the countries they'll be visiting and where they might find them. Canned beer, for instance, generally isn't sold in foreign hotels. Planes and trains, however, are a terrific source of foreign cans. In fact, during the late 1950's, European air and rail routes—particularly those which crossed international borders—were just about the only place to get foreign beer cans. Many of the cans were imprinted with "Specially canned for B.O.A.C.," "Packaged especially for Lufthansa," and other identifications.

The very least your Aunt Nellie can do for you on her return flight from the Riviera is ask a stewardess to save her a bagful of all the foreign cans consumed on the journey. The stew will almost always oblige.

If you find yourself with a little time to kill in a foreign brewing city and can bluff your way through the language, try visiting the brewery. Phone ahead first. If you play your cards right, you may pick up an old can, or at least a couple of current ones. When collector Bill Christensen visited an Austrian brewery once, he was told that Kaiser Pils was canned for export only and wasn't sold in Austria. He asked if they had an empty can or two and was told, "No, but would full cans do?" He went home with a six pack of this excellent beer.

In the past few years, more and more countries have started canning beer and ale. Each year sees some 200 new brands or designs, and foreign cans are finally being sold in quantity in America. But no matter what people may try to tell you, foreign beer in cans isn't a recent phenomenon. According to the Tin Research Council, England began experimenting with canned beer in 1936, and England, Scotland, the Isle of Man, Germany, Holland, Canada, Mexico, Puerto Rico, and Venezuela have all produced cone tops.

* * * *

Once you have visited every liquor store and supermarket in your state, your search will take you to the great outdoors—or, more exactly, to the dumps. Whether you check out your local municipal dump or an unofficial roadside eyesore, you'll be helping your environment at the same time you add cans to your collection. Open dumps are scarce today in most urban or suburban areas, but they still abound in rural backroads areas. The warmer and dryer the climate, the better preserved the cans will be. Even in areas which have hard winters, you may find some cans buried in the mud and preserved from the elements.

In combing through a dump, you'll probably have to work your way through about 20 years of modern refuse to get to the goodies. Most of what you uncover—if you find any beer cans at all—will be in deplorable condition, but you may find a gem here and there. Even cans which look pretty bad at first can often be cleaned up considerably and turned into respectable display cans. Fortunately for the collector, cans from the 30's and 40's were solid affairs, well coated with protective lacquers. They often survive the elements in much better shape than more recent cans in the same dump.

Before you head out for the nearest dump, put on old clothes, boots, and gloves. Dumps are often home for rats, snakes, and other animals you probably wouldn't want as pets. Take along rakes, shovels, and plenty of plastic bags. If the dump is private and posted, be careful. A rusty beer can isn't worth a tail full of buck shot or rock salt. Well, *most* beer cans aren't.

The average dump won't be a thing of beauty when you arrive, but there's no law that says you can't leave it looking better than it did before you started digging. This is particularly true of roadside dumping spots. Why not remove the rest of the trash along with the cans? Although this should be reward enough in itself, you might get some publicity in your local paper and scare up a few more cans from people who read about you.

If digging in dumps sounds involved, that's only because it is. But it can be a lot of fun. Take a friend along and get into the spirit of adventure. Make it a family affair. The cans you find won't be pristine, but they're better than nothing. You can use them as traders, and you just might find a brand that was previously unknown.

Dumps aren't the only source of cans. All you have to do is keep your eyes open. Several collectors have made big hauls in abandoned railroad stations where the freight clerk spent more time drinking beer than dispatching freight. Maybe that's why so many stations are abandoned. Some people have even found cans in vacant lots, parks, can companies, or the homes of former can company employees. And, scattered here and there around the countryside, are untold numbers of can collections, boxed up and sitting in the attic, just waiting for you to climb up after them.

HORST WENDLAND [Canada] and JOHN VETTER [Virginia] meet on the floor of the lobby of the Netherland-Hilton in Cincinnati to trade cans during Canvention III.

Dump digging, house hunting, and station searching are all solitary means of gaining new cans for your collection. You will probably find, however, that the fraternal method—trading—is the quickest way to build your collection. But before you start trading, first build up a stock of duplicate cans. Although saving the other five cans in a six pack is second nature to collectors now, it hasn't always been so. The first time Bill Christensen and his father went out to buy different brands of beer, they came home with—among other treasures—eight six packs of cone tops. Naturally, they threw away all but one of each brand. Bill still has bad dreams about that mistake, but who would have dreamed back then that there were other people crazy enough to collect empty beer cans?

Collectors know now, though, that there are thousands of other people out there just as crazy as they are—not to mention a few sane ones—so they save their cans. So, they store traders away, usually washing them thoroughly first.

You have to do something to turn those extra cans in the garage into cans on your display shelves, so you type up a list of all your traders and send it to another collector asking him if he needs any of them. Some of these lists are quite detailed, sometimes including Polaroid snapshots of the cans. Most are photocopies or carbons, although a few collectors with access to computer equipment actually send their lists out on print-out sheets.

If the collector who receives your list sees any cans he wants, he jots them down and sends you his own list. More bargaining may be necessary, but within a couple of weeks you should each receive the cans you needed.

An active mail trader keeps pretty busy carrying packages to the post office, but it's always fun to see what's waiting in the mail after work. It's not uncommon to add 500 cans to your collection this way in a year.

If you're the outgoing type, as most collectors are or have learned to be, you'll also want to try some face-to-face trading. The collector living along a well traveled highway or near a popular tourist attraction receives frequent phone calls from fellow collectors passing through town who want to stop by for a couple of beers and some trading. Collectors who live in the same town naturally often get together to trade some cans. But the most most effective means of face-to-face trading in the BCCA are chapter meets and, of course, the annual canvention.

However they choose to trade, most collectors use a set of BCCA guidelines which recommend each type of can's trading value in terms of current cans. Any can in general production now,for example, is worth any other can currently sold. A recent obsolete can is worth two current cans, while most cone tops are worth eight currents. The list goes up to obsolete U.S. gallons, which have a recommended value of 20 current cans. There are many exceptions to these guidelines. For instance, nobody with a rare 007 can to trade would think for one moment of accepting a Ballantine's Ale and a Buckhorn for it. Most collectors get around a dilemma like this by trading a cone top for a cone top, a quart for a quart, a current for a current, and so on.

* * * *

Now that you've gone to all the trading sessions and have searched through every dump, trash can, fraternity house, warehouse, tavern, barn, bordello, cellar, attic, campground, old brewery, and vacant lot within a 1,000 mile radius of your home, what are you going to do with your treasures? There's no doubt about it—beer cans take up space. But they don't take up as much space as bottles, so your wife can thank heaven for small blessings. If you want a collection that doesn't occupy a lot of space, try stamps. But who wants to collect something you paste into a notebook and hide in a locked file drawer? Maybe you can't mail letters with beer cans, but you sure can stack them on shelves and make a decorative, colorful display. Cans are ready indicators of advertising and marketing tastes over the years, as well as the mute witnesses to all the smaller brewers that have sadly fallen by the wayside. If you're proud of your collection, show it and spread the faith.

Most beginning collectors stack their cans pyramid-style on a convenient table or shelf. You might try this for awhile, but after your three-year old accidentally knocks them over the fourth time in a day, you'll look for another way of displaying them. Some collectors show their cans in well-lit, glassed in cases. Others put them in plastic six pack holders, stack them one on top of the other, then run a metal rod down the middle of the six packs. Some even stick cans to the walls of their dens with two-way adhesive strips.

The most common way to display collections, however, is to build special shelves. You can spend hundreds of dollars on elaborate shelving, or just a few dollars for something plain but functional. One advantage of shelves is that, unlike most other display means, they make it easy to rearrange your collection as you add new cans. Most collectors display their cans in alphabetical order, so when they come home from a trading session with 40 new cans, it's easier to slide cans around on shelves than it is to rearrange a pyramid.

Some collectors arrange their collection alphabetically by state, but this can lead to many label duplications. You could display nine current Busch Bavarian cans, and they'd all be the same, with the exception of the brewery's location.

When you're displaying your cans, you'll also find the visual effect is significantly enhanced if you open them from the bottom. Use an old "church key" opener. The intact top looks much better on your shelf.

With all its searching, sorting, bartering and displaying, beer can collecting can be both relaxing and competitive, decorative and ecological. It's inexpensive—a student or blue collar worker can have a better collection than a professional person. By trading through the mail, you can form lifelong friendships with people you've never met. Or you can go to a canvention and make hundreds of friends in just a couple of days. And while you're doing all this, you can enjoy a cold beer—from a can, of course.

Mark Olson of Williston, North Dakota, constructed his neat shelves from pine.

"DUMPING FOR BEER CANS"
By Clyde L. Hooker #2985, Bimidji, Minnesota

I first started collecting beer cans about twelve years ago when the hobby wasn't known to as many as it is today. I didn't really get bit by the "can bug" badly, however, until about 1971. In June of that year, with not too much money in my jeans, I bought an old '49 Chevy (motorless) half ton pickup truck for $50.00. This would be my "can wagon". After many hours of body work, my boys and I felt we had done a pretty good job for our first crack at such work. While we worked, my son-in-law was overhauling a big Chevy engine he had bought for $25.00. By September, we had it all together and ready for the road. We added dual stacks, fog lights, outside diesel truck air cleaner, a super-charged engine, split manifold, and a four-speed transmission. I felt I was ready to go after the beer can.

I have often been asked where I find the can. I can best answer this question with one word: "Everywhere!"

When I started to collect beer cans seriously, I made a promise to myself to put both heart and soul into the hobby. I lived with the beer can on my mind during the day, and I must have gone to bed with it on my mind, as my wife told me more than once I mentioned something about beer cans in my sleep. I skipped meals, gave up all TV, and a lot of sleep. It even got to the point where I would shun company and close friends every chance I got just to use the extra time to hunt the can.

Finally, I realized that I was neglecting my loved ones and I took a long look at what I was doing. I realized that my wife was playing second fiddle to the beer can and that I was pressing my 14 year old son into hunting with me, leaving him little time with his friends. I've now regained some of my senses, so now we hunt cans only when the spirit hits us. I now find myself enjoying can hunting more than ever but without the old pressure. I had been in a beer can hell, but I proved that I can beat the devil!

My son Si and I are holders of 65,000 plus beer cans! We have about 200 foreign cans, around 20,000 cone tops, about 4,000 silver growlers and crowntainers, around 30,000 flat tops, and the rest are tab tops.

We've found these cans as close to home as a neighbor's beer party, and we have driven as far as 200 miles for them. We must have driven over 5,000 miles to get the cans we have. Most of the cans we have we found ourselves, although I've traded for about 1,000 of them. We have been to hell and back to lay claim to a lot of the cans we have. Mile after mile, I've forced the old truck down roads that once were traveled by horses and oxen, pushing through mud four to eight inches deep, fighting snow and ice up to two feet deep. We've been stuck in snow drifts and once walked 22 miles to get help. Si and I have fought bitter northwestern gales from Canada with their snow, sleet, and misery, all for the want of the beer can. We once were run up a tree by timber wolves and had to stay until some trappers came along. We have fallen through the ice, getting chilled to the bone. I once walked into a quick sand hole and, if not for my son, would not be here today.

Very often, while can hunting, you'll come upon a dump that has cans so far gone that you walk away in dismay, wishing that you could have found them five or ten years ago. But, don't walk away just yet. Over the bank lie a couple of old car bodies, old doors, piles of old roofing or shingles, and maybe a bunch of old siding. Look in and under these before you go and nine times out of ten you'll find a few almost-mint cans. Many a time I have found near-perfect cans in the glove compartments or under the seats of old junked cars.

When you are out for that Sunday drive, be sure to stop at bridges, overpasses, and other roadside hideaways. Many good cans have been thrown there and they're still there if some other can nut hasn't beaten you to them.

Don't overlook lovers' lanes. These are a must because some of them date back to when you and I were still sparking. Wish I had all the cone tops I threw away back then.

How about skid row? Ever look around there? Those old buildings have cans in them! Get down in the basement if you can; I once told a landlord I was interested in buying an old store building and got a chance to look the place over. I found 64 flat tops in mint condition in the basement. I felt so bad about that little trick that I sent him a buyer some time later.

Try roadside rest areas for out of state current cans. One time, heading to the southern part of the state, I came to one and headed for the first garbage can. I lifted the cover and started digging. Nothing there, so I went to another one about fifty feet away. I had just started digging through the second can when a little old lady came up to me and asked me how long it had been since I last ate. "Oh, back up the road about thirty miles," I answered.

Another way Si and I have found some nice cans is the "lookout method", as we call it. Si stands up in back of the truck and I drive. This way, he can see in the ditches better. When he wants me to stop, he hits on the top of the cab.

We generally carry beer with us when we're out can hunting. When we can't seem to locate any good dumps, we sit down and I sip on a beer. It's good and relaxing, and one must be relaxed to think. Think of the people who lived here. Were they beer drinkers? Most dumps were put down wind from the house. Since the wind is mostly from the northwest up in this part of the country, I cast my eye to the East, South, or Southeast. Next, I take a survey of the close terrain to give me some idea of old garden spots and paths. Look for the old outhouse, as many times the dump would be nearby. Look for a ravine close by that might have been used for dumping. Look for old roads thatled away from the building site. Nine times out of ten, you'll find a dump along the road or at its end.

Resorts are a great place to look for cans. You'll find lots of cans that tourists brought with them. And, watch those trash cans.

Sometimes, when we're driving country roads, we stop at farm houses, especially when we see the farmer in his yard or field. We put our can story to him. Most farmers have their private dump, and if you use the right lines, you might strike it rich. I always greet the farmer first and praise his cows, pigs, and corn to get him in the right mood. Then I pop the question.

Up in our area, we have many places to look for cans you may not have where you live. We have old logging camps and lumber mills, many fire trails, and logging roads to hunt on. We are known to have 10,000 lakes in this state, and if you figure there are a few resorts by each lake, you come up with a pretty good number of dumps.

A fellow from Chicago once told me my can dumping was successful mostly because of the area in which I lived. Hogwash! If I lived in Chicago, I could have a ball can hunting. I'd watch for the guys that collect the trash and offer them a little token for their trouble if they'll keep their eyes open for unusual brands. Next, I'd head for the dumps and country roads just outside of the city, look

for "no dumping" signs, and start looking. Cans are every-where—just use your head. Ever since the first beer was put out in cans, men have been dropping them at their side or giving them a little toss. On some of the older cans you'll read "when emp-ty—throw away". . . . .many people did just that.

Have any truck driver friends? I have one, and he has brought me cans from eleven different states.

I also have a friend who's a maid at a Holiday Inn. She saves any unusual beer cans she comes across while cleaning rooms.

I have many cans, and there are few that I have found without some help or a friendly tip from someone. And since very few of us have the gift of reading the other fellow's mind, we have to let him know how he can help us. Ask, and nine times out of ten ye shall receive.

In my short lifetime of fifty-one years I have seen a lot of fads, fancies, and hobbies come and go, but I can truthfully say that beer can collecting (and hunting) is one of the fastest-growing that I have seen. Beer can collecting is still in its infancy, and I sure hope I'm around when it gets into the adult stage of its cycle.

My field experience has been a great and wonderful educa-tion—one that no school teaches. I have learned a lot of man and his ways while in search of the beer can. I have learned patience and perseverance, and to the small collector and the beginner, I say, get acquainted with those two words.

Yes, we have been to beer can hell many times. Si and I have drunk the bitter draughts of beer can hunting. We share many little personal secrets together that only he and I would be able to understand and believe. We lived them together and it is the one thing that no one can take from us. Sometimes, while sitting around the house, my son or I will say, "Remember that so and so can?" We'll remember, sometimes with laughter and at other times with a far away look in our eyes or almost a tear. The rest of the family does not understand this or our ways, but we don't expect them to. As I said before, we've been down that road together.

BCCA TRADING ETIQUETTE

It is impossible for the club to officially police trading by members as we have no authority to do so; however, it is felt that the following rules or suggestions might well be heeded by all in order to keep as many people as happy as possible.

1. We are in this for the fun of it, the main fun coming from getting new cans for our collections. Thus, don't enter into any trades except in good faith and there should be no problem.

2. The main responsibility of the trade should lie with the initiator of the trade. Do not contact someone about a trade unless you yourself can expect to follow through promptly and fairly. If a member is not interested in making a trade when contacted, it should be common courtesy to return a quick rejection reply. Such a note can be easily attended to in less than five minutes. When sending out trading lists, don't list cans on your trading list that you do not have in your possession. . . too many people are counting on liquor store stock as their trading list. . . if you don't own it, don't list it!

3. When a trade is entered into, the obvious major difficulty is that, in most cases, we are unable to see the actual cans involved. Pictures are a great help here, but in most cases we must live with written lists, some of which are more elaborate than others. Since the major difficulty in this area seems to be the condition of cans, it should be everyone's concern to mention any flaws in cans [obvious great problems being excessive rust, horrible dents, squashed by a car, full of machine gun holes, or full of unknown bugs]. Some members prefer to use a 1-5 grading system here, with 1 being very good and 5 being hardly worth displaying. The main point. . . *unless you say otherwise, the person with whom you are trading is going to expect a good can!*

4. While every trade is really the responsibility of the two traders, it is suggested that there should be much more being done in the way of approval trading. By this, it is meant that should two traders be unable to come to a satisfactory agreement once some cans are sent, some or all cans might well be returned by one or both parties.

This should thus prevent people from being uptight over having gotten the bad end of a trade. Should anyone feel that they are unhappy over the trade, they should not hesitate to let the other party know so. Furthermore, if anyone is approached in this fashion by a member following a trade in good faith, he should consider it his responsibility to rectify the situation. Here the approval idea can easily be used, wherein a can might be returned, or another might be given to "even-up" the situation.

5. A few people have had difficulty with the question of postage in mail trades. For the most part, this should not even be anything worth worrying about, since overall postage should pretty well even out. In some unusual situations, however, a member might offer to pay postage, such as a case where he might desire to see a quantity of cans strictly on an approval basis, and the other party agrees to send.

6. Can values also seem to be a source of concern of late, since some are, let's face it, simply worth more than others. The problem. . . even advanced collectors can't make a perfect assessment of can values. As a suggestion only, therefore, collectors may wish to use the following list of values for cans. This is primarily for the benefit of members who are new, confused, or want to settle an argument! It is in no way binding, but a good guideline by which we can all operate. There is no reason that a member should not consider a particular can worth more (perhaps due to known scarcity—Soul M. L. ought to be worth more than 2, for example) or less than these suggested values. Also, there is no reason why a member might not want to trade a particular can except for a can of similar value, age, or scarcity—or even type! This is not always possible, of course, so the following list is expressed in terms of current cans. All values are mainly expressed in terms of top condition cans, though the older they are, we might well expect to put up with a little more in terms of rust and so forth. Still, one would logically expect to subtract an appropriate value amount for cans of lesser condition.

UNOFFICIAL SUGGESTED VALUES—in terms of current cans

    1 = current cans, all sizes through 16 oz.
    2 = recent obsolete cans from the 60's and 70's.
    2 = foreign cans, including Canada, Mexico, etc.
    4 = obsolete cans from the 50's, obsolete foreign.
    6 = obsolete cans from the 40's [must have Internal Revenue Tax Paid].
    8 = all cone tops [those from the 30's may be worth more].
    8 = obsolete cans from the 30's.
  10 = WWII olive drabs, due to scarcity.
    8 = current gallons.

16 = foreign gallons.
20 = obsolete U.S. gallons.
16 = obsolete quart cone or spout tops.

A final word on the above. Some members may feel that such and such can may be worth much more [or, unlikely, much less]. Keep in mind that due to the rapid growth of can collecting, we are entering into a period where inflation could run rampant unless we all decide right now that we ought to prevent this. We all know what has happened to the economy in general. No need to have that happen to us. The above list is very *sensible* even if not exact, in terms of current can worth. Remember, if members decide to needlessly inflate can values, they, in turn, can expect to pay an exorbitant trading value to someone else in the near future, with only themselves to blame for driving up values to the point where they will eventually become absurd.

7. There is no excuse for the failure of some members to respond to a series of letters by one party when a trade has not been resolved. In this situation, a member should feel free to write the club through the club address, and the Board will send a fair warning letter to the person who is not living up to the trade. If after an additional 30 days the matter has not been resolved, or the cans returned, further complaint by the original complaining member will then cause the announcing of the offending trader's name and number in the next ensuing News Report, so that all members may be aware that this person is a poor risk in a trade.

8. Due to our large membership, keep in mind it is impossible for everyone to make the most favorable trades. Luck, and even hard work, will play a great part in the trades we all make. Good sportsmanship is of the essence, and every member should be willing to make appropriate consessions in good spirit if needed.

9. The following recommendations to members are not to be considered as requirements or demands of any nature but purely ideas which members may wish to use. If you have any suggestions, send them in to National Headquarters and perhaps a formal sheet of standards can be compiled and sent to each member. You may incorporate some or all of these suggestions when sending your trading list to other members.

A. When possible, cans should be opened from the bottom.
B. Cans are assumed to be in good condition unless otherwise noted on list.
C. Foreign cans should be listed separately from U.S. brands.
D. List should be in alphabetical order.
E. Unless otherwise noted on trader's list, all cans are assumed to be 12 oz.
F. When possible, list the year can was purchased over the

retail counter.

G. Cans should be CAREFULLY packed for shipment to prevent damage in transit.

BEER CAN ABBREVIATIONS

TYPE OF BEER	TYPE OF CAN	CONDITION OF CAN
A Ale	AA All Aluminum	GC Good Condition
B Beer	AT Aluminum Top	FC Fair Condition
BB Bock Beer	CT Cone Top	PC Poor Condition
D Draft	SL Seamless	CP Current Production
GB Ginger Beer	TT Tab Top	OP Obsolete Production
NB Near Beer	FT Flat Top	OB Out of Business
ML Malt Liquor	SS Solder Seam	D Dent
P Porter	WS Welded Seam	R Rusty
ST Stout	ES Epoxied Seam	VR Very Rusty
MLA Malt Lager		W/OT Without Top
		W/OB Without Bottom
		Res Restored

"Internal Revenue Tax Paid"
March, 1950 is a clear demarcation date for beer cans. All U.S. cans filled before that date were required by the federal government to include the above wording somewhere on the can.

OFFICIAL BCCA CAN GRADING

GRADE 1 EXCELLENT
Mint to near-mint condition. Has top and bottom, but may have "church key" holes in top or bottom. No rust, scratches, fading, dents or easily noticable imperfections on any sides.

GRADE 2 GOOD
In good condition. May have shallow surface scratches, small nicks, slight "dimples", but no rust on any sides. A good display can.

GRADE 3 AVERAGE
In good shape, however, may have some easily noticeable light rust, scratches, nicks, "dimples", fading, etc. May have good front, poor back. Good enough for most displays.

GRADE 4 FAIR
Just barely good enough for display if you're not too particular — but needs replacement if a better specimen comes along. Has defects of Grade 3 but more severe. Perhaps restorable to Grade 3.

GRADE 5 POOR
Rusted or faded and lable is undistinguishable or almost so. Not suitable for display or trading and not restorable to a higher grade. Get rid of it!

by Bill Christensen #33 et al

HOW TO BOTTOM OPEN ALUM' CAN FOR BEER DRINKING

BY Mr Malt Duck #.007

USE A SHARP BEER CAN OPENER - MAKE FIRST HOLE FROM EDGE OF CAN IN A STRAIGHT LINE TO THE CENTER

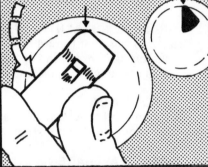

THE OUTER EDGE OF THE CAN IS STRONGEST SO USE IT FOR A PIVOT POINT MOVING THE OPENER LIKE ABOVE

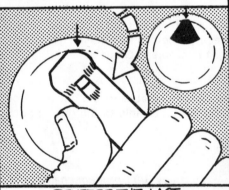

REVERSE THIS LAST MOTION WITH THE OTHER HAND FROM THE OPPOSITE SIDE

PUNCH SMALL HOLE IN OTHER SIDE OF CAN AND YOUR READY TO GET AT THE GOOD STUFF INSIDE !

DEVELOPED BY THE RESEARCH DEPT. OF THE HAPPY HOPS MUSEUM OF BEER CANS BY MR. MALT DUCK

Diamonds From the Dumps
Restoration and Preservation

With a little skill and the tools that most do-it-yourselfers already have around the house, you can often create masterpieces out of those dented hunks of rust can collectors so fondly call "diamonds from the dumps."

SUGGESTIONS FOR CLEANING DUMP CANS

First Step: Get those cans. However, you'll soon learn that every can isn't worth dragging home. Cans with very heavy rust probably will not clean up, but don't be too quick to pass up rare cans. The best advice is to try a few rusty cans on your first trip. You'll soon recognize the ones which are too rusted to restore.

Second Step: Wash all cans with soap (or any laundry or dishwashing detergent) and water. You needn't do a perfect job. The oxalic acid solution you'll use later will remove some of the really tough dirt. This is only a first cleaning to remove the heavy dirt.

While washing, try to shake out as much dirt, leaves and other foreign matter as possible. Be careful—this "foreign" matter may well include ants, spiders, snakes, and even mice. (This is another reason to clean the cans the same day you bring them home. It avoids infesting your house with various creatures of the dump.) Repeatedly filling the can with water and vigorously shaking it out will help. All cans should be wiped dry with a soft towel. Do not settle for letting the cans drip dry as many parts of the country have water characteristics that will deposit agents to cause rust or other types of corrosion to the paint on the can.

Third Step: You won't have to acid treat all cans. Separate the cans—those which are mainly just dirty, but not too rusty, and then those which have unattractive rust. Take the first group back to the wash bucket and this time really work on them with soap and water, perhaps using a toothbrush gently on the stubborn spots.

Fourth Step: Once you've selected your cans for acid treatment, you're ready to prepare your solution. Now, what will you use?

1. Oxalic Acid. This strong acid attacks rust but does not bother paint. (However, it does tend to fade out the yellow colors if cans are left in too long.) Oxalic acid is a poison, and must be kept away from the eyes. It shouldn't stay on the skin too long. Use rubber gloves, ice tongs, or some such aid in handling your cans. To mix the powered acid, try: 1 qt. of water (hot or cold, but watch it. Hot acid cleans cans in 1 or 2 minutes and will damage the can if it's left in longer) to 3 medium tablespoons of acid. This will make a medium strength solution. You may have to experiment with even stronger solutions (more acid or less water) or with weaker solutions (more water or less acid).

2. Various cleansers containing oxalic acid. Zud and DuPont Cooling System Cleanser are examples of this type of product. With DuPont, for example, mix about 1 oz. of the cleanser with 3/4 qt. of water. Again, you may want to experiment with stronger or weaker solutions. Some collectors use citric acid.

Fifth Step: The cleaning. Mix your solution in a plastic, metal or glass container. You might punch two small holes in the top and bottom of the can so that it will sink in the solution more easily. If you do not wish to punch additional holes in your can, then simply pour some of your acid into a second container, set the can in the acid container, and fill up the can as you pour the acid back into the cleaning container. CHECK THOSE CANS FREQUENTLY! About every five or ten minutes isn't too often. Some cans may stay in the solution as long as overnight with no harm done. Again, experience will help here. If you leave a can in too long you may damage it or ruin it, so it's smart to practice on some cans of lesser value.

Sixth Step: When the desired amount of rust is removed, or at least when the can seems "finished," get another bucket and put in about two gallons of cold water. If you mix this water with baking soda, or some commercial neutralizing agent, you will neutralize the acid. Otherwise the acid may continue to work on the can and eventually damage it. After a minute or so, remove the can and dry it. You may still need to wash carefully to get some last bits of dirt off the can.

Removing Dents

Some diamonds from the dumps have perfect labels, but have fallen prey to the can cruncher, that so-called he-man who proves his masculinity by mercilessly squashing empty beer cans (and after all they've done for him!). These cans may look hopeless, but some simple restoration work can make them prizes in anybody's collection.

Dent removal is possible in several ways with probably the simplest being to drop a small firecracker in the can, letting the force of its explosion remove the dent. This may work on small dents, but is not successful when the dent is of a more serious nature. Caution— don't try the firecracker method on aluminum cans!

Minor dents also are sometimes forced out by filling the can with water and placing it in the freezer. When the water freezes it expands, thus, removing the dent. Be careful that the can isn't left in the freezer too long or the ice might expand the can too much, resulting in bulges.

It is possible to remove dents of the larger variety with air pressure. This, however, requires making a clamp-on type jig that will insure holding the air pressure inside the can. A home made clamp can be made from a short piece of heavy-duty radiator hose which would be of the size to fit over the open end of the can and clamped tightly with a radiator hose clamp. The other end of the hose would have an adaptor clamped on it with a quick coupler air hose connection. Pressures up to 125 P.S.I. can be applied to empty beer cans, but this should be done slowly because a quick rush of air pressure might cause the can to rupture.

The can should not be held in the hand when the air pressure is applied. By the same token, do not use an old or inferior hose as you will find it will not hold up under pressure. Keep the hose as short as possible, insuring against the hose rupturing under pressure.

Some serious dents can be removed with the "Dr. Pepper method". It seems that the 12-ounce Dr. Pepper bottle fits perfectly inside a 12-ounce beer can. Thus, you merely remove the bottom of the dented can, force the Dr. Pepper bottle into the can and pound out the dents with a hard rubber or wood hammer. In some cases the can will be too dented to ease a Dr. Pepper bottle into and we suggest you use a pipe of smaller diameter. Place the pipe in a vise and hammer the dents as you roll the can around the pipe. Sometimes both ends of the can may have to be removed before starting this procedure.

Replacing Tops and Bottoms on Cans

Often, old cans have been discovered where one end has been removed with a can opener so the can could be utilized for drinking, storing nails, and so forth. With a little skill and practice, most anyone can become adept in performing this type of restoration.

The first step is to remove the remainder of the original lid (rim). This is done by slowly and carefully using a grinding wheel to grind through the lid rim. Once you have ground through this metal, the rest of the ring may be removed with pliers.

Now you must cut a small amount of metal from the end of the can to bring the can to proper height. This is done best with a pair of Wiss M-5 Compound Tin Snips. Measure the proper height and then scribe a line around the can at that point by using a sharp scratch awl assuring a straight line by wrapping a metal strip around the can at the point where the line is to be scribed. When cutting off the excess metal, cut a light bit above the line. After the metal has been trimmed, use a fine file, laying flat across the opening and rotate the can slowly as you file. Next, to insure a good fit, it is best that you use a very smooth file to sharpen the can to nearly a knife edge. This is done by applying the file on an approximate 45° angle rotating the can as you file. This will make it easier to slip the can onto the new end.

Next, take another can with a good top and cut through the body of the can about one inch from the top. Now, crimp the one inch remaining so it will fit into the can that is being restored. The crimping can be done with pliers or, better still, a Malco Hand Crimper which can be purchased at a tool supply firm that caters to the heating industry.

Once the crimp has been made, you need only insert the crimped piece into the can being restored and tap it in place with a wood or hard rubber mallet until the can end seats flush on the filed end of the can.

In the case of cone tops, a top from a gasoline additive can such as Heet or STP can be used. For a bottom, use the bottom end of an aerosol spray can, most of which have a concave bottom as do most cone top beer cans. A word of caution: puncturing aerosol cans may be dangerous. Be sure all the gas propellant is expelled before puncturing the can. This can be assured by holding the spray button down until the hissing stops, then puncturing a small hole with an ice pick to release the remaining gas. To add tops and bottoms to cone top cans, follow the same procedure as with flat tops.

This writer has not, as yet, developed a method for restoring tops or bottoms to necked-in and drawn tin and aluminum cans.

Making Cans by Hand From Can Company Flats

The making of cans from flats (the printed sheet metal before it is rolled and a top and bottom added) is becoming more popular as the beer can hobby continues to grow. Most flats, never having been exposed to the weather, are in mint condition and are valuable additions to any collection. Many experimental brands of beer which never reached the market are available only in this form.

This type of restoration is the most time-consuming and requires the most amount of metal working skills. We will describe two methods of seaming cans; the "crimped" seam and the "lapped" seam. We'll first discuss the lapped seam.

The first step is to trim the flat to proper dimensions. In most cases this will mean trimming the height only; the length is usually correct, and the same amount of metal is required for a lapped seam, which we will describe, as is required for the clinched seams used by the can companies.

Measure carefully the distance between the top and bottom rims of a manufactured can; this distance plus 1/16" is the measurement to trim your flat for height. It is very difficult to do this by hand; you could take your flats to a local tin shop and have them do this for you. Care should be taken to remove an equal amount from the top and bottom as cutting all from one end would, in many cases, destroy a portion of the label.

The next step is to roll the flat; you should also have very old flats rolled at the tin shop, as they are very hard to roll by hand. The older and thicker flats have a tendency to show creases if not professionally rolled. The newer flats from about 1960 on have become thinner and are easier to trim and roll.

If you wish to try your own rolling, try rolling a flat over a 12-ounce Dr. Pepper bottle or a piece of 1½" diameter pipe. They need not be rolled to a perfect diameter as the later steps of this process will insure proper diameter and symmetry of the can. Proceed to roll slowly without forcing the metal or creases will develop. If creases do appear, do not be concerned as they can be rolled out after the seam has been soldered before the ends are installed.

You now will need two drawbands (radiator clamps) approximately the diameter of the can. Place the drawbands around the partially rolled flat, one near each end with the two new ends placed in position. Be sure to put some felt between the clamps and painted surface of can. The drawbands are then tightened until fairly snug, but not to the point that the ends cannot be removed.

In this position, use a small electric soldering iron to tack solder the seam at the top and bottom of the can. Do not attempt to solder the entire seam as the heat will cause it to buckle and the job will be botched. Now remove the drawbands and also remove the two ends.

The next step requires another special device—a clamp to hold the seam from buckling while the balance of the seam is being soldered. We recommend a special home-made clamp similar to the one shown in the illustration. Install this clamp and solder the seam. After removal of the clamp wash all remaining traces of soldering acid from the can with soap and water to prevent corrosion.

Now, all that remains is to install the two ends and you have created a masterpiece! Earlier in this chapter we described how new tops and bottoms may be added to a can—follow those same basic steps in finishing up your can.

The crimped seam probably takes more time to make, but will give your flats a smoother, more finished appearance. As with the lapped seam, you must first trim your flat. Standard flats should be 8 3/8 inches long to insure proper diameter and seam, while cone top flats need be only 8 1/2 inches long. It is not necessary to trim the length unless it is significantly over these measures.

Once trimming is complete, lay the flat, label up, on your work bench. The unpainted seam area on one end will be wider than it is on the other. Using a ruler and a sharp instrument, scribe a line 1/16 of an inch from top to bottom along the wider edge. Turn the flat over and repeat the process on the narrower end.

Next, tightly clamp the narrower end under a steel straight edge, leaving only the 1/16 inch area exposed. Three-inch C-clamps are recommended for each end and a larger clamp for the middle. This last clamp will have to be applied from the rear of the flat, so it is best to work on a thick board protruding from your work bench.

Bend the exposed area of the flat's end in toward the straight edge. Crease it with your fingers and remove the large clamp. Then tap the crimp with a hammer to even it out and close it. Remove the flat from the clamps and reinsert it label up. This time, bend the crimp toward the label. Repeat the creasing process and remove.

Roll the flat carefully around your two-inch pipe (it gets a lot of use) and hook the crimps together. Making sure the crimped edges are completely aligned, hammer them flat against the pipe.

To bring the two portions of the seam you have just created into the same plane, insert a hacksaw blade between the rolled can and the pipe. Make sure that the top of the blade (the non-serrated portion) is under that part of the can forming the lower part of the seam (the part that had the crimp bent back toward the face of the flat). Holding the can in position manually, hammer along the seam to form a ridge along the blade. You should now have a really professional-looking seam.

All that remains now is the installation of a top and bottom using the method described earlier.

REPAINTING CANS: ANOTHER FACET OF RESTORATION

Once the dents have been knocked out and the rust removed there remains the question of what to do with those big areas of bare metal or those faded-out letters on our prized Brew 17s and Hopping Toad Malt Lager cans.

The obvious answer is, of course, to touch up or repaint those blemished areas. Not all of us have great artistic ability, so here are a few painting tips.

    1. Don't try to work wonders. Don't try to repaint everything. Do only what you, limited by your own skill and experience or lack thereof, can. This may mean just touching up the black or red lettering of the brand name and forgetting about the

faded-out background or striping. We've all seen badly repainted cans, and they should have been left alone!

2. Use a good brush or brushes. This may sound minor, but it isn't. Don't try to save a few cents with a dime store brush; you'll find it losing hairs right in the middle of the S in Soul. I'm partial to red sable artist's brushes and find that the most useful sizes for this work are a number 2 for background work and 00 and 000 for finer work. These will run you a buck or three apiece, but it's well worth it.

3. Use good paints. On newer, shinier cans, modeling enamels such as Testor's or Humbrel's work well; just don't put them on too thickly. If they dry too shiny, rub your thumb over the painted area, and the combination of friction and skin oils will dull it sufficiently.

   On older cans I prefer flat lacquers, and I've found Imrie-Risley Military Colors to be particularly good. Unfortunately, these are not cheap (about 75 cents per 1/2 ounce jar), but they do brush well—something not all lacquers do. If these colors appear too flat when dry, a clear, semi-gloss can be applied over the entire can. If you do this, make sure the repainted areas are *completely dry* or the paint will "bleed."

4. Match your colors correctly, and match the degree of "shininess" correctly. Some colors are easy to match: black, most reds, and most greens and blues. This is essentially because most beer can colors are quite basic rather than oddball shades. White is a very difficult color to match. You may be better off repainting the entire white area and using an off-white or ivory. Most white paints are too white for beer cans. Silver and gold on early (1930s) painted cans may be roughly matched. Here again, use a very high quality gold or silver paint. The Imrie-Risley's are good. Shake thoroughly to get a good suspension. Apply sparingly, and, when the paint is 98 per cent dry, use the trick of rubbing your thumb over it to blend with the surrounding area.

   On modern cans, silver and gold generally are not painted—they are plated. You cannot duplicate this without an expensive electroplating outfit and a lot of technique. Don't even try to paint it—it will look terrible. Leave it as it is, or, if you insist on doing something (here again there is a cost factor) get a jewelers' hand held miniature buffing wheel or a modelers' wheel. For silver or gold stripes, hold the wheel against a straight edge held on the can (you will, naturally, need three hands for this.) Run the wheel along the straight edge and buff yourself a stripe of bare metal of the desired width. Clean off the can to remove paint and metal dust; then apply clear gloss lacquer over the stripe for a silver stripe or clear, thinned, yellowish spar varnish over the metal for a gold stripe. 'Tain't perfect, but 'tain't bad either.

Regarding the matching of shininess: I have seen many cans ruined because some well intentioned soul put a high gloss paint as a patch on a can where the paint was faded and dulled. It sticks out like a sore thumb. If anything, the gloss or lack of it is *more* important to getting a good match than is the exact shading of the color.

5. This may sound simplistic, but hold your hand steady, and work in a good light. If you think something is beyond you, don't even attempt it unless it's a throw-away practice can.

6. Be very careful with masking tape. Cans which are faded enough to require major repainting are generally sufficiently deteriorated so that the bonding of the paint to the metal is no longer good—even if the can is not bubbly. If you put on tape, you may find yourself with swaths of bare metal when you remove it. If the can is bubbly, *forget about tape.* I've tried tape and ruined a couple of moderately scarce Yoerg's crowntainers in the process. In addition to pulling the paint off, I also found the poorly bonded paint is liable to seepage via a sort of capillary action—a hopeless mess.

7. Be sure one part of the job is thoroughly dry before proceeding to the next. Work on a group of cans at once, and do a bit on each while the others are drying.

8. Take good care of your brushes, and they'll take good care of you. You paid good money for good brushes so don't ruin them. After each color, clean them thoroughly. At the end of each session, clean them doubly thoroughly and then rinse under very soapy warm water. Leaving the soap in the bristles, shape and repoint the brush and allow to dry.

9. If you make a blunder, painting over a line or whatever, don't try to rub it off right away (if it's a small blooper). This will smear it into a larger blooper. Let it dry, then flake it off with a pin.

10. Finally, don't try to con anybody. There's nothing immoral about repainting a can—it's just another form of antique restoration. . .but don't try to trade a can as original paint when it's a product of your own workshop. I sign my work on the bottom of the can. The ethics of restoration are a ticklish business. Some people prefer pristine rust (Note: Such people also generally like organic vegetables, the rhythm method, and Plantar's warts.) On the other hand, The Metropolitan Museum of Art in New York City paid more than a million dollars for a Greek vase which it purchased as a shoe box filled with about 150 broken shards and fragments.

Museum officials glued it back together, and, horror of horrors, *repainted it.*

A   B   C

D   E   F   G

PHOTO CAPTIONS

A. The simple faded-out letters, one color repaint. On this can, the OE of TAHOE had faded out completely. The red color is easy to match.

B. A slightly more difficult one-color repaint: The dark blue borders around the name Peter Doelger had faded out, as had the word "First". Here again an easy color match, but requiring a relatively steady hand.

C. The difficult color white: Here in the brand name as well as the field on the bottom third of the can, an ivory color was used to restore the paint.

D.   An advanced one-color repaint. On this Berverwyck can the green on all the label and lettering had almost completely faded out after the can was forgotten in an acid bath over a weekend. The underlying silver color of the can and brand name was not repainted, just the green around it.

E.   On this Valley Brew can there were large rust patches on the left hand side (viewer's right). These were repainted with silver, which was then smudged (as described in the text).

F.   The complicated patch-job. This Duquesne can had a large blotch of thick brown paint on the lower right (viewer's left) where someone had previously tried to repaint it. That was stripped off, and the area was repainted with a thinner brown color which matched the color of the can. The black woodgrain was then painted in. Then the yellow stripe was restored. Lastly, the words Pittsburg and Copyright were repainted.

G.   The multicolored repaint: This Eastside can had faded and rusted almost completely. The goat was repainted free hand. Then the brand name and the words Bock Beer were done in dark blue, then the word Genuine and the inner oval in scarlet. This was followed by the outer oval in mustard yellow, then the can body itself in greenish brown, and, finally, the word Zobelein's in off-white. This was a difficult job because of the intricate free hand work, the large number of colors, and the fact that many unusual shades had to be mixed to get a proper match. It required about 11 hours and is not recommended for the novice.

Preservation

Perhaps the simplest, but not the easiest way to protect a can collection is to wash the can periodically as you would other things in your home to keep them looking new. This would be a lot of work!

There is much controversy over the use of wax; some faithfully wax every can with furniture polish or other waxes. Others say "forget the wax, it'll turn yellow in time." This writer feels that some type of protective coating is desirable in maintaining a can collection in its best possible condition over a long period of time.

Collectors will differ in opinion as to what product is best, but this should be up to the individual and what he or she prefers after some experimentation. Waxes will, of course, give your cans a shiny appearance but some will argue that beer cans shouldn't be too shiny.

Spraying cans with clear plastic is a good method of preservation, but might tend to be a bit expensive. This method creates less shine than wax, but only time will tell if this plastic will eventually turn yellow.

After talking to many collectors on the subject of protective coatings, the consensus is that the majority will stick to cleaning cans periodically with soap and water, but a strong minority believe that the combination of cleaner and wax products available are best to keep your collection looking sharp. There are even some who argue that it is right to let the cans achieve a normal aging process as older cans should reflect age and not have a shiny new look.

* * * *

Restoring and preserving "diamonds from the dumps" can be a most satisfying pastime. If you don't already have them, purchase the tools mentioned in this chapter and give restoration a try—you'll be proud of the results and it will add many hours of relaxation and enjoyment to your hobby.

The 12-ounce Dr. Pepper bottle fits perfectly inside most 12-ounce beer cans. To remove minor dents, merely force the bottle inside the dented can and lightly pound out dents with hard rubber or wood mallet.

This picture shows two radiator hose clamps holding "flat" in position for spot soldering top and bottom.

Wiss M-5 Compound Tin Snips — recommended as best for use in restoring beer cans.

This illustration shows top and bottom of "good" can which have been cut about 1" from rims and crimped with Malco Hand Crimper.

This picture shows can before and after dents have been removed.

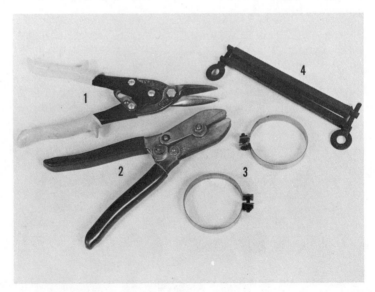

Tools necessary for restoration: 1. Wiss M-5 Compound Tin Snips, 2. Malco Hand Crimper, 3. Radiator hose clamps, 4. Homemade seam clamp.

by Gil Brennell #13 et al

A Hobby, not a Business

Many collectors, unknown to each other five years ago are now among the thousands of proud members in the well publicized Beer Can Collectors of America. People who years ago bought a can of beer only because it held a tasty, cooling beverage, now buy the can for the can alone — and sometimes never even taste the beer. The collector who once saved only one can from each six pack or case is now saving them all—one can for himself and the rest for trading.

Today, the lowly beer can has taken on assorted values according to its availability, year of manufacture, size, country of origin, type, numbers distributed, and condition.

As the hobby has grown, some collectors have started buying and selling cans. The BCCA opposed this; to understand the reasons behind these efforts, you must first understand the thinking that went into organizing the club.

The BCCA's original reason for existence was to "aid members in enlarging their collections." It was set up as a hobby, and as such, the means for accomplishing this end was to be trading with other collectors. The trading was to be done on a social basis. There was no reason to outlaw buying and selling of cans at this time since the small group of original members didn't believe in it.

When the organization was still young and small, there was no place for profiteering since early trade sessions were actually "give away" sessions among friends with the only guide being, "If you see it and need it, take it." But two things happened to change this type of feeling, both stemming from the rapid increase in new members.

At local trade sessions, the many new members meant part of the small family spirit was gone. With the loss of familiarity, a more stringent type of trading came into being. Secondly, the BCCA began to accumulate members from all corners of the United States. This, of course, meant easier availability of almost all current cans. Consequently, with more collectors—each building up a stock of local cans for trading—it became necessary to find obsolete cans to have something different and unique for trade interest. This put the premium on obsolete cans, which are hard to find. When this happened, existing members who were at least half-way active, could, in a very short time, accumulate almost all of the currently available cans. But if they wanted obsoletes, they had to put in some time and work to locate them.

But what about the established member who ran across a motherlode of obsolete, but not too rare cans? Chances are that most of the established members already had that particular can and wouldn't trade for another. The newer members, unless they were extremely fortunate, didn't have enough current cans to trade for the older can.

So, the alternatives: the collector could hold onto them and slowly trade them as the opportunities arose, trade them for other traders, or he could attempt to sell them. So, the active soliciting of BCCA members to purchase cans began. It was easy—the BCCA had no formal rules which said it was illegal for a member to buy or sell cans. And there in the roster was a complete list of potential buyers!

At this same time, another factor was coming into play. As a city inherited more and more beer can collectors, it also inherited more people looking for beer cans. The first collector to stop in at a given antique shop or flea market may or may not have found some cans. The second collector received a polite response that there were none to be found in the shop. When this process was repeated by a number of collectors, the shop owner soon became aware of a potential profit-maker. With no idea as to what constituted a desirable beer can, these outlets began to build up a supply of currents, recent obsoletes and a few older cans. Not knowing what price tag to put on them, they began to charge whatever the market would bear.

The interest in beer can collecting began to accelerate at about the same time that a larger overall category of collecting also started to accelerate. In the early 1970's, the "Nostalgia Boom" erupted. This craze encompassed the collecting of virtually all items from the '30 s, '40 s and '50 s. Beer cans, which originated in the '30 s, were carried along with the overall boom. Many will recall the coin collecting boom of the early '60 s when such words of encouragement as, "they're not making any more of this type," caused both the number of coin collectors and coin prices to skyrocket until the saturation point was reached. At that time, the number of collectors declined and, along with it, the so called premium value of the coins.

As the BCCA grew, interested members and the club officers warned new members that there were some who would sell cans, but that the club frowned on the buying and selling practice. There was no rule or amendment in the constitution or by-laws yet, so members were left to judge and act for themselves as far as getting involved with profiteers.

However, in late 1973 and early 1974, due to the active solicitation of members by "can merchants," the club began a campaign to halt profiteering and profiteers.

After several cases of flagrant profiteering, some involving just a few members, others involving mass mailings to mostly newer members, the BCCA's Board of Directors decided to try for legislation that would lock out the profiteer. Therefore, at the third annual canvention in September 1973, the following resolution was presented to the members:

"Buying and selling of any beer can or non-official club item at any official club function shall be strictly prohibited. Club meetings shall be held for the fun of swapping, comradeship and the conducting of club business. Any member buying or selling beer cans, beer related items or non-related items, shall be subject to removal from the premises and subject to forfeiture of membership."

By an overwhelming majority, the resolution passed and was incorporated into the by-laws as Article V. It quickly became apparent, however, that this resolution was not strong enough for it covered only club members and only at "any official club function." Since the only official club function each year was the canvention, the amendment's power was quite limited.

The Board of Directors, realizing the inadequacy of this article in dealing with profiteering, sent the following proposed addition to the by-laws to the membership for approval in May 1974.

Subject: MEMBERSHIP

WHEREAS, BCCA has been founded with the intent of increasing the interest in the collection of beer cans, and WHEREAS the basic intent of this organization is to build a hobby on the principal of fun so that all people of all ages and income may participate on an equal basis, and WHEREAS it is our objective that no one through membership in BCCA should receive any personal profit through the solicitation and the sale of beer cans by the use of the membership roster, membership in BCCA shall be granted with the following understanding:

Membership is open to anyone who has an interest in collecting and maintaining a display of beer cans, empty or full. The type of collection and display shall be at the sole discretion of the individual member. How each member obtains his/her cans shall again be at his/her discretion, but it should be understood that the buying and selling of cans among members is strongly discouraged. It is urged that every member improve the individual collections by trading with other members, thereby helping someone else while helping themselves. Unsolicited offers, in any form, by a member to another member to sell or buy cans shall be strictly prohibited and anyone so doing will be subject to forfeiture of membership. A membership roster shall be made available to each member for his personal use. The membership roster is made available to facilitate communication between members. At no time should any member give, loan, sell or barter any original or copy of the current or outdated roster to any non-member. Anyone so doing will be subject to forfeiture of membership. All alleged violations of this amendment shall be referred to the Board of Directors. It shall be the responsibility of the Board to verify all allegations, and if verified, the Board shall be authorized to revoke the membership of the guilty party.

By a vote of 1139 in favor to 75 against, the amendment passed; its passing made it virtually impossible for all but the most determined profiteer to gain access to prospective customers. At the same time, it eliminated any chance of profiteers actively working from within the club at any time during the year. These initial steps should effectively combat profiteering in any club or organization if correctly applied by each collector. Each must police his own sphere of influence, especially in his or her own methods of collecting. At the same time, each individual collector should do his best to help educate the newer member-collectors to the relative values of the beer can and discourage any affiliation with can merchants. Only in this way will the hobby continue to flourish as a hobby and be prevented from becoming a source of profit for a brotherhood of profiteers.

The BCCA has never, and will never, attempt to dictate what anyone can do with his or her own time and money. The club has set up certain regulations only when the activities conflict with the intent of BCCA rules and are carried out in conjunction with BCCA activities. The club admits that beer cans have a value, just as every material object has a value.

However, the BCCA's members want a club where the monetary value doesn't obscure the fun and enjoyment derived from building a collection. Allowing the dollar to command priority would mean the more affluent BCCA member could have the best and largest collection simply by buying cans. It is the desire of the majority of the members that the scrounging, digging, hunting, and trading is an integral part of beer can collecting, and that eliminating these methods would destroy the fun as well as the friendship they invariably create.

The philosophy of the club is based on these principles;
1. Increasing the interest in the collection of beer cans.
2. Building a hobby in which all people, of all ages and income, may participate on an equal basis, and;
3. Making sure no one receives personal profit from the solicitation and sale of beer cans.

Perhaps this editorial from BCCA's *News Report* of January, 1975, sums up the club's basic feelings in regard to buying and selling of beer cans:

Congratulations on your birthday! Back 40 years ago your parents, afraid of what the neighbors in Newark would say, decided you should be born in another town. Yes, even before birth, you were not trusted. On January 24, 1935 the announcement of your birth appeared in THE RICHMOND NEWS LEADER. Most said you would not live long. But you did.

Through the years you have matured to new sizes, shapes, styles and colors. You dressed in olive drab and helped us win World War II. You've slaked the thirst of many a hard-working American. You've spread your good to millions of people the world over. You have served well.

You have not always been treated kindly, old friend. You have been punched, pulled on, kicked, bent double, misprinted and thrown into ditches to fade and rust. You have been cussed while the one who abused you got off scot free. Some have even tried to ban you from their states.

For 40 years you have endured much pain, mistreatment and misunderstanding. But you have stood up to the test. You have fought a good fight. You have grown more sturdy and beautiful with age.

Only in recent years have a comparatively few people discovered your true beauty, dignity, personality and depth. But, those people, in honoring you and your heritage, have stirred the minds of those who are drawn by the evil dollar like the 49rs of the 19th Century. They want to buy you and sell you, not for your beauty or renown, but for their personal profit.

Meek friend, faithful servant, whether new, old, rusty, shiny or faded. . . . .wherever you may be. We love you!

BCCA has, in a few short years, grown from a small group of six collectors in St. Louis to an organization encompassing thousands of enthusiastic collectors in every state of the Union, plus foreign countries as well. It's a natural target for those who seek a quick dollar. Such people do exist, but the BCCA's history proves you can maintain fun and interest without succumbing to the draw of the dollar.

by Henry Herbst #70 and Bill Henderson #73

A Few Interesting Cans

"That Eastern with the skyline of Chicago on it is one beautiful can," said Kenny Jerue. "How many cans do you want for it?"

"Just one," the other collector replied. "A Pikes Peak by Tivoli—*that's* one beautiful can."

Jerue didn't have a Pikes Peak by Tivoli to trade, so the deal fell through.

But the question remains: Is the Eastern from South Bend, Indiana, rarer than the Pikes Peak from Denver's Tivoli Brewery?

Even with thousands of collectors swapping beer cans—and beer can stories—there's no real agreement as to which are the rarest cans.

Matter of fact, there's not even much agreement as to how many different cans have been made. Some insist there are no more than 12,000; others say there are over 20,000.

And the most publicized "tough" cans probably aren't the rarest at all. To be well known, there have to be enough of them around so that a fair number of collectors have them—and talk about them.

The really rare can is the one that a collector finds and then can't find out anything about from his fellow collectors—including how rare it is.

One thing all collectors *do* agree on, though, is that a lot of very interesting cans have rolled out of America's breweries in the last forty years.

Yes indeed—from ABC to Zody's, with many fine collectible names in between. Blue Boar Ale. Cloud Nine. Gilt Edge. Golden Gate. Nu Deal. Paul Bunyan. Simon Pure. Spearman Straight Eight. Tivoli (spelled backward, it's "i lov it"). Tube City. Tru Blu. Wooden Shoe.

There are beers and ales for every letter in the alphabet.

The first, of course, was a K. For Krueger. Krueger Cream Ale, the green can that began it all in 1935. (Green, incidentally, continues to be the most popular color for ale cans.) You'd think the first can made would be a very desirable one to have in your collection, and you'd be right. But another early can from the same company, Krueger Bock, is even harder to find—*much* harder, say the experts.

Another Krueger first, it should be noted, was the 16 ounce can, which the pioneering firm introduced in 1941.

The first of the major brewers to can its beer—if only on a limited basis—was Pabst.

Pabst made its move in July of 1935, six months after Krueger broke the ice.

Pabst didn't want to risk the reputation of its Blue Ribbon Beer in the new containers, though, so it cautiously entered a test market (Rockford, Illinois) with a canned beer bearing the Pabst Export name. The handsome silver and blue containers are among the most common of the early beer cans.

Within a year, the other two brewers that make up today's Big Four were also in cans: Anheuser-Busch had offered its Budweiser brand in a flashy gold can and then tiny Coors was advertising Coors Golden BEER in a can surprisingly similar to its current Coors Banquet can.

(Many of the early cans carried the word "BEER" in huge letters, probably because people at that time weren't accustomed to finding the beloved beverage in a metal container.)

As a matter of record, most collectors like to have the big brands of today in their cans of yesterday, but numerous lesser brands have better stories going for them.

Take Hals Beer, from Baltimore. Its can design was inspired by the famous Dutch portrait painter, Franz Hals, who was known for his pictures of noblemen drinking and carousing in tavern settings.

Another beauty is Hitt's Sangerfest (song festival). This defunct brand (Pueblo, Colorado) carried the words of favorite barroom tunes like "Drink to Me Only With Thine Eyes," "Coming Through the Rye," and "Camptown Races."

One of the great small breweries on the West Coast, the Sacramento Brewing Company, makers of Buffalo Beer, survived prohibition by making Buffo near beer, then reintroduced Buffalo in what are now highly desirable cans just a few years after the Eighteenth Amendment was repealed.

Another curious aspect of the brewing scene on the West Coast is the Happy Hops phenomenon. Although the brand bearing this name has been obsolete for quite some time, several of the other Grace Bros. brands carried a Happy Hops emblem for many years thereafter.

Other hoppy beers that have poured onto the scene over the years include Hop Gold (Vancouver, Washington), Hopsburger (Oakland, California), Hop'n Gator (a citrus/malt liquor melange from Pittsburgh), and Bullfrog (Chicago). According to famed collector Ernie Oest, "They call it Bullfrog because it's got hops in it!"

A goodly number of beloved beer brands are deeply rooted in local pride. Like P.O.N. (Pride of Newark) Ale, Lager, Porter & Stout from the now-defunct Feigenspan Brewery. (In 1939, the firm could boast that P.O.N. Ale was the biggest selling ale in N.Y.C.)

Another proud beer is P.O.C. (Pride of Cleveland). This set of initials also stands for "Pilsener on Call."

The District of Columbia once had a beer of its own, Senate.

Today, most of the lawmakers who drank it are gone—and so are most of the cans. A valued collectible.

The nation's 50th state has had a beer of its own, too: Primo. Now made by Schlitz, it's the only beer ever canned in Hawaii. (Alaska, it must be noted, is one state that has never produced a canned beer.)

Little Staten Island's only beer in cans was R&H Staten Island Light Beer, and many a BCCAer would be willing to swim to the island to get his hands on one.

Local pride knows no boundaries. A case in point is the Jax can from New Orleans that proclaims: "It's Go Texan Time Again. Jax Salutes the Heritage of the Proud State of Texas."

In 1970, A-1 beer (Phoenix) put out a special commemorative for Arizona's 100th birthday. It, too, is one beautiful can.

Cans that have been made, but never or barely issued, will drive any collector into a frenzy of lust.

One such item is the Rainier Ale can that was only on the market for one run. It carried a lengthy description of how well it was made on the back, but the Washington State Liquor Board took exception to some aspect of it, so Rainier (Seattle) went to a can design without the offending verbiage.

Anheuser-Busch, tinkering with the idea of offering a popular-priced beer, has provided collectors with some rare packaging treats. Busch Lager, made from March, 1955, until sometime the next year, is a highly desirable can. More so than the beer was, it's said. Seems the brewery was experimenting with artificial carbonation on this brand—and that had a lot to do with its falling flat.

Even rarer are the six plain Busch Beer (not designated as lager) cans that were only offered in test markets to determine the relative strength of each package design. None was ever produced in any quantity and Busch Bavarian finally wound up as the giant brewer's only representative in the low-priced segment of the marketplace.

The famous and infamous have given their beers a special panache. Grand Prize (Houston) was produced by the Howard Hughes-backed Gulf Brewing. Manhattan Premium, All Star, and Canadian Ace are all known to be the products of Al Capone's Chicago brewery. (Manhattan beer—in Chicago?)

Neither famous nor infamous is the bearded Ben whose picture appears on Uncle Ben's Malt Liquor (Canada). It is said that Ben was wearing a false beard when photographed, and has since grown a real one to live up to his image. Literally.

When you hear a collector talking about "gag beer," he may not be referring to the quality of the brew. Instead, he may be talking about the joke beers that have come out every once in a blue keg.

A modern classic is King Snedley's (San Francisco). Lucky Brewing very calculatingly created the brew to go after the 18-25 year old market because they felt their other brands didn't cover it well. A put-on, the can carried the line "Beer With Us" and showed cartoon portraits of King Snedley, Princess Fatoona, and others. A tongue-in-cheek advertising campaign exhorted the youth of California to "look for the royal family on the can." Interestingly enough, the beer inside was not Lucky Beer. Instead, it was specially brewed to compete with Coors and Oly and did, in fact, beat those brands in a taste test conducted with college students. Nevertheless, the beer went bust after a six-pack of months or less. But if the 18-25ers didn't go for King Snedley's, thousands of collectors sure do.

Another brand that has enjoyed great status among collectors is Olde Frothingslosh (Pittsburgh). The pale stale ale (as it is known), the beer with the foam on the bottom (as it also is known), began as a figment of disc jockey Rege Cordic's imagination on KDKA. When Cordic's crazy commercials for the nonexistent beer scored with his listeners in 1954, the funloving Pittsburgh Brewing Co. slapped zany

Olde Frothingslosh labels on 500 cases of Iron City bottles and gave them to officers and friends of the brewery.

The next year, it was made available to the public, too—as a holiday season specialty. The 12 oz. version was all in bottles, but there was also an 8 oz. can called Sir Lady Frothingslosh.

Although 10,311 cases of Sir Lady were sold that year, less than one case is known to still exist.

Sir Lady was never seen again, but 12 oz. bottles of Olde Frothingslosh continued to appear during the holidays until 1968. That year, a 12 oz. Olde Frothingslosh can made its appearance.

The next year—and for several years thereafter—it was bottles only again, so all who had been lucky enough to obtain the '68 can prized it highly.

And then, in the winter of 1973, the value of the 12 oz. Olde Frothingslosh can took a real nosedive. Pittsburgh Brewing reissued it—in huge quantities—as a poptop. And then, the following year, the same design once again was offered—in several colors, yet!

If Fatima, 1968's "Miss Olde Frothingslosh," "chosen for her beauty, talent, poise. . .and quantity" is a throwback to some other age, a couple of cans have hit America's beer coolers that are decidedly spaceage. Orbit beer, for example, comes to us from Miami, only a hop, rice, and barley from Cape Kennedy. And then there's Astro, "The first stout malt liquor brewed to give you that cool lift required by people of the space age." Astro is from California. Naturally.

Try as they may, neither have the beauty (or rarity) of the two Cook's Goldblume conetops from Evansville, Indiana, that feature the old sidewheelers, Cherokee and Robert E. Lee.

A set of two, however, is pretty puny stuff compared to the really prolific can designers like Schmidt, Iron City, and the like.

Schmidt (St. Paul) came out with about seven outdoor scenes in the mid-50s. Not counting Schmidt Draft or 16 ouncers, the set grew to 17 during the next decade. Then, in the early 1970 s, another four scenes were added.

Meister Brau (Chicago) also put out a series of ten "happy day scenes" a few years back. And Rainier (Seattle) came out with its gigantic jubilee series. Figuring all the combinations of color and design, there must be a total of 300 different cans in the set. Drewry's (South Bend) has also produced a plethora of cans over the years —including the horoscope series, the character series (tells all about you based on the shape of your face, ears, etc.), and others. Drewry's ran many of its designs through in different colors, so the total number in this series also is boggling.

When beer can collectors talk about boggling numbers of cans, however, the name most likely to come to mind is Iron City. In addition to the Frothingslosh fun and games cans, Pittsburgh Brewing has come up with an Iron City can to commemorate just about everything that's ever happened of note in their sales area. With more than five dozen cans issued by 1975, many collectors figure that 5 per cent of their collections are Iron City commemoratives of local landmarks, historical events, seasonal scenes, or teams like the Pittsburgh Pirates, Steelers, or the University of Pittsburgh.

Of course, making special cans to carry schedules, records, and team rosters is not really rare in the beer canning business. After all, the brewers know which side of the TV set their beer is drank on.

Altes Sportsman Ale, a late-50's offering from Detroit, carried sports facts. A sampling: "Ty Cobb led the American League in batting 12 years." "Carp have reached the age of 75 years." "7 out of 10 Michiganders drink Michigan-brewed Beer or Ale."

As you can see, some of the sports facts were sportier than others. Other sports-oriented cans include: A-1 carrying the schedules of the Roadrunners and Phoenix Suns. Colt 45 with the Golden State Warriors schedule. Gambrinus (Pittsburgh) with the success of the '74 edition of Ohio State emblazoned thereupon. And Carling Black Label's special issue for the Boston Bruins Stanley Cup victories a few years back.

One college team even inspired a brand new *brand* of beer! After a perfect 10-0 record, the Billy Cannon-powered Louisiana State University team of 1958 developed so much enthusiasm among the populace in its home state that the Jackson Brewing Co. of New Orleans brought out Tiger Beer. After a few months, sales declined as the fervor waned. Eventually, Tiger died. A few nice specimens now reside on the shelves of collectors, but not many.

Another sought-after can in the sporting genre is Cook's 500 Ale. Created for distribution during the Indy 500, the can shows a race car and a checkered flag. It was produced only in the 50's and is, therefore, almost as hard to get as the winner's trophy.

The same holds true of Fehr's ("It's always Fehr weather!") X/L in

the "Silver Bumper" (Crowntainer) with the race horses in full gallop all the way around the can. A Louisville beer, it's assumed that this version of the X/L brand was produced to coincide with Derby Week.

More assumptions: Many collectors believe that Twins Lager (Duluth) is related to the baseball club of the same name. Others think Dodger Lager (Los Angeles) was made for distribution only at the ball park. If they're not right, they should be. Another example: HOME RUN. . . The Malt Liquor that struck out!

If you have a Home Run Malt Liquor can in your collection you are indeed lucky. It has become one of the most wanted items by can collectors. . . . . probably because of its name and scarcity. It is a very well designed can with black and white printing on a gold background. This brand was brewed and sold in Puerto Rico only.

This colorful brand was introduced in October 1969. They named it Home Run for two reasons. First, to correspond to its strength. Second, because Puerto Ricans are perhaps the biggest baseball fans in the world (Yes, even more avid than we on the mainland). Only a total of 13,000 cases of 10 ounce cans were produced and the brand was removed from the market in February, 1972.

The brew was made by The Antilles Brewing Company and was the first malt liquor made in Puerto Rico. Why was it taken off the market? Simple. . . it didn't sell well enough! Apparently, Puerto Ricans have not acquired the taste for malt liquor. Particularly adverse to the products were the bar owners who quickly realized that it was far more profitable for them to sell two or three beers to a customer than one Home Run.

When the heavy hitters sit down to talk about beer can sets, three that originated in Philadelphia are sure to be mentioned as the very toughest to get. Just getting a single can from any of them, in fact, is an achievement worthy of recognition.

From Esslinger, which closed in '64, there are the the famous Parti-Quiz cans. Produced from '56 or so through the early '60 s, in various color and design mixes, there are believed to be at least ten varieties of the Parti-Quiz can. They bear fabulous facts like: "Mississippi Won the Cotton Bowl in 1956." "Napoleon was 'Little Corporal.'" "Moon revolves on own axis." "Snakes' Teeth are Called Fangs."

Desirable? BCCAer Doyle Davidson once had three stolen from his hotel room by someone lower than a snake's tooth.

Another superset is the Tooner Schooner series from Wm. Gretz Brewing. The company, which went out of business in '61, will live forever in the hearts of beer can collectors—and music lovers—for the fourteen cans which carried the words to such tunes as "A Hot Time in the Old Town Tonight," "Casey Jones," "Take Me Out to the Ball Game," and "Sweet Rosie O'Grady."

Another Gretz series—any can of which would bring a smile to the collector who came across it—is the "G.B. Fleet Car" series. The back of each of the cans in this series carries a line drawing of a sports car the brewery would've liked you to believe it had in its garage.

No single brand has caused more controversy among can collectors than Soul. Soul was brought out in Watts during the riots, say some. Actually, the two Maier-brewed Soul brands (Soul Malt Liquor and Soul Mellow Yellow) were distributed in late 1967, *two years after* the disturbance; 550,000 cans of each (half 12 oz., half 16 oz.) were made in all—American Can Co.'s minimum private label order.

And yes, it *is* hard to get, but not impossible. In fact, BCCAer Cacti Pete had a couple of cases of it for trade at one time.

Only two other black-oriented cans are known: People's and Black Pride, "A beer as proud as its people." Both come from Wisconsin breweries.

Packaging beer so that it will appeal to a specific group, of course, is pretty common.

A classic case is "calorie-controlled" Storz-ette (Omaha), the "original beer for women." Did the 8-ounce can (which carried a picture of an orchid) control calories merely because of its size? No matter. This late-50's brew stands alone as the Virginia Slims of the beer packaging business.

And, on the other side of the bar, there's Mr. Lager. Boasting that it's "For Men Only," this Fox Head product (Waukesha, Wisconsin), like its sister brew, Storz-ette, hasn't been produced for several years.

Of course, Storz-ette is only one of a long line of beers that have offered themselves to the public claiming low caloric content. One of the first was an early can of Acme Beer (LA & San Francisco) which boasted "Non-fattening refreshment" right there on the front of the can. Later, the can was revised to read "dietetically Non-fattening." As with many brands, the cans reveal how the lawyers had to revise claims to suit the Feds.

Meister Brau Lite (Chicago), which has now become just plain Lite (Miller Brewing), has over a dozen can designs behind it to show how the legal tinkering with the calorie claim evolved over the years.

The same is true of the other major brews that have tried to give us the idea that their product won't add to our already substantial beer bellies: Mark V (Columbus, Ohio), Gablinger's (New Bedford, Massachusetts), and Dawson's Calorie Controlled Ale (ditto).

Health claims have been illegal in promoting the sale of alcoholic beverages for some time in the U.S. That's why it's fun to look at the fine print on the original Pabst Export can: "It is safe, pure, wholesome." Probably the most outrageous health appeal any beer has ever made, however, is that of Schlitz Sunshine Vitamin D Beer.

If you can't make health claims on your beer can, what kind of claims *can* you make? Several brewers have gotten a gleam in their eyes and have come out with girlie cans.

Probably the most desired is the James Bond's 007 Special Blend series. (The "special blend" is beer plus malt liquor.) In a six month test in 1970 by National Brewing in San Francisco, Knoxville, Phoenix, and Jacksonville, a total of 18,000 12 oz. cans featuring four girls in seven basically different can designs were distributed. Many collectors wish it were 180,000.

Another toughie in the girlie category (or any category, for that matter) is Playmate by the now-defunct Sunshine Brewing Co. of Reading, Pennsylvania. Produced in two versions, beer and malt liquor, Playmate's alluring big eye design dropped out of sight when Hugh Hefner started threatening suit for infringement upon his property. The result was a rare pair of cans any BCCAer would love to get his hands on.

From hot to wholesome: The Miss Rheingold contest ran in the New York area for many years, but in only one of those years did Miss R. appear on a beer can. The year was 1957. Before the voting took place, each of the six contestants was publicized via beer can (truly a modern mode of communication). Later, when the winner was determined, she appeared on a special can commemorating her victory—(Diane Baker, who went on to become a movie star, was one of the runners-up whose picture appeared in the sixpack.) Rheingold never again put its contestants on beer cans. And, in fact, the contest was soon discontinued when the promoters couldn't find a way to cope with the race situation. (They are alleged to have felt that if they nominated a black girl, she would get all the black votes and win for sure. Rheingold would then become known as the beer for blacks.

And if they didn't nominate a black, they'd be branded as prejudiced. Either way, they stood to lose a chunk of the market.)

No discussion of girlie cans would be complete without a tip of the beer mug to Tennent's Lager, from Glasgow, Scotland. The Tennent's 12 ouncers (there are 20 in all) show various lovelies being lovely. The interesting thing about all this is that these cans are for export only. They're not intended to be sold in their native land. Which just goes to show something or other.

And then there's that porno beer. Yes, porno beer. It's another export-only brew. A product of the Graenges Breweries of Graengesberg, Sweden, the cans bearing the naked ladies and naughty words are marketed just in Denmark. Last December, more than 120,000 of the controversial cans are reported to have been sold in Copenhagen alone!

Among the most controversial domestic cans would be those that bear the proud name, DuBois Budweiser.

This Pennsylvania brew finally had to drop the Budweiser monicker when they lost a lawsuit to you-know-who.

(DuBois often seemed to have delusions of grandeur. An early can bears the legend, "DuBois, the perfect beer." Elsewhere, the same can claims that DuBois is "Brewed with clear, clean, top o'the mountain water." How much water, the collector asks himself, can you find on top of a mountain?)

A survey of nearly any collection of beer cans will turn up a number of look-alike cans. A common example is Wiedemann Bohemian Special. For a number of years, this Midwest brew bore a startling resemblance to Bud. Ironically enough, where Bud has a line running up the side that reads, "GENUINE," the Wiedemann version substituted the word "ORIGINAL." Now we know!

Other look-alikes include McLab/Salzburg and K&J Private Club/Wisconsin Private Club.

Talk about confusion! Warsaw Brewing of Chicago caused a whole lot of it when they bought Burgermeister cans from the defunct San Francisco brewery, filled them, and slapped their own brand, Bergemeister, using a paper label yet!

The tops of the cans, of course, still bore the familiar BURGIE of Burgermeister.

Paper labels are unusual in the canned beer business, but not unheard of. Others that have used them include Primo, Schlitz Malt Liquor (embossed, even!), and a Gluek Stite cone top.

A paper label on a cone top of course, *is* a rare combination.

Any cone top for that matter, is reasonably rare. That's why many collectors don't evaluate a collection by the overall number of cans it contains. "How many cones do you have?" they'll ask.

Among the most common cones are Grain Belt (Minneapolis), Champagne Velvet (Terre Haute), Berghoff 1887 (Fort Wayne), Falstaff, and Schlitz.

Krueger—the first beer in cans—had cone tops for awhile, too, but its first cans were flattops.

Because cone tops are so desirable, some collectors have created them from conventional flattops with a little solder and the top off an STP can. Usually, they do it as a joke (a Hop'n Gator cone top?!), but every now and then, someone tries to pass one off as the real thing.

To most collectors, the other major category of cans-much-to-be-desired is gallons.

It is believed that fewer than 30 U.S. brands have been packaged in the oversized containers. The most sought-after include Brew 102 (Los Angeles), Blitz Weinhard (Portland, Oregon), Koch's Deer Run Draft Ale (Dunkirk, New York) and Gettelman Bock (Milwaukee).

Only two Gettelman Bocks are known in collections (John Ahrens and Bob Myers, both Falstaffs of the beer can collecting fraternity, are the lucky ones).

But even *they* have to look up to Will Anderson, for he has what is believed to be the one and only Grace Bros. (Santa Rosa, California) gallon in existence.

Interestingly enough, some beer cans have tried hard to hide their existence.

Those, of course, were the camouflaged cans of World War II. Among the brands that donned the drab tones of olive to—it is hoped—protect the drinking/fighting man were Schaefer (Brooklyn), Carling's Black Label (it should have been Green Label), and Fort Pitt (Pittsburgh).

They were, respectively, a flat top, a cone, and a Crowntainer.

Another colorful rarity is the bright green Schlitz that may or may not have been made for St. Patrick's Day. If it was, it's a genuine tough can. If it was just a freak of lithography, it joins the jillions of mistake cans you can find rattling around in the trash barrels of any canmaking company.

Some beer cans have been produced in extremely limited numbers—and yet virtually every one is in the collection of a member of the Beer Can Collectors of America. Those, of course, are the BCCA commemorative cans, issued each year during the annual canvention.

The 1973 can—much to the delight of the canventioneers—was a cone top!

The 1974 edition, a striking black, gold, and silver can designed by Kent Eggleston, was the organization's first lithographed commemorative. (All previous canvention cans were silk screened.) 3,264 of the '74 cans were made.

For the record:

Another very special can around canvention time is the Can of the Year. Selected by a vote of the BCCA membership, the recipients of this honor have been as follows: 1972—Fyfe & Drum (Rochester, New York). 1973—Our Beer (Monroe, Wisconsin). 1974—Colorado Gold Label (Pueblo, Colorado). 1975—Acme (San Francisco, California).

The '74 winner is from a segment of the beer can market that accounts for a great number of brands—but only a very small percentage of the beer sold in this country.

House brands, they're called. Or private labels. Supermarket chains often have them. So do large liquor stores—and big drug store chains in states that permit them to sell beer.

Colorado Gold Label, for example, was made by Walter (now defunct) in Colorado, but sold primarily through Thrifty Stores in California.

9-0-5 is among the better known private labels. Made especially for the 9-0-5 liquor stores in the Midwest, the brand got its name (as did the stores) from the street address of the first store in St. Louis. At last count, there were 36 stores in this Pet, Inc.-owned chain.

A sampling of some of the other major store brands you'll find in cans:

Grand Union, 7-11, Bohack (Giant Food), Maid Rite, Schwegmann, Prize (Food Fair), Brown Derby (Safeway), Finast, Tudor (A&P), Shoprite, Shopwell (Daitch), Hynne (Fed Mart Store), and Crystal Colorado (for Von's Supermarket chain in California).

Of course, anybody who is willing to put up the money can have his own private label. To wit: Park (for Park Beverages, New Jersey), Jennings (for Jennings Liquors, Minnesota), Katz (originally for Katz Drugs, now for Skaggs' Drugs in the Kansas City and St. Louis area), G.E.M. and G.E.X. (for the discount stores for government employees), Hoffman House (for Harry Hoffman, Denver's first and the nation's second largest liquor store), Dart (for Dart Drug), Astor (for

Home Liquors), Golden Valley (for a liquor store in Golden Valley, Minnesota), Ski Country (for Foss Drugs in Coors' hometown, Golden, Colorado), and Sternewirth (for Otto's Liquors in Mendota, Minnesota).

A lot of beer has gone over a lot of bridges between Krueger's brave entry into the canned beer business back in 1935 and Otto's Liquors very own house brand up in Mendota, but one thing is very clear to anyone who would screech to a stop at the glint of an empty beer can along the side of the road.

Any can you don't have is a tough can!

by Lew Cady #98 et al

Travel Guide

For the beer can collector, a supermarket or drugstore in a distant state can prove as valuable a treasure trove of cans as an old dump behind an abandoned tavern. But hunting for new cans in another part of the country can be frustrating because liquor laws vary widely from state to state, and even from county to county or city to city within a state.

In most states, commercial liquor stores are good places to buy local brands. Tennessee and New York, however, don't sell beer in these establishments. And several other states have government-controlled liquor stores which don't sell beer. State stores in Iowa and Washington, though, do sell malt liquor.

Grocery stores are almost always a good source of local beers. As we noted in Chapter Eight, many chains even have brands bearing their own name.

In your travels, you might enter a half dozen groceries in a particular state, only to discover that food stores don't sell beer there.

This can happen in Delaware, Illinois, Maryland, North Dakota, Pennsylvania, Rhode Island and often in other states. Generally, a travelling beer can hunter's best bets are liquor stores, large chain stores, most grocery stores, "beer docks," party stores, carry-outs, and drive-throughs.

Taverns, for the most part, sell only national brands or common local ones, usually at a high price. Many charge extra for cold beer. Drug stores in many states sell beer, but here again the selection is often limited. In some states discount stores and service stations sell beer.

Beer hunting in Pennsylvania offers a particular challenge, since only two places—beer depots and taverns—sell beer. At depots you have to buy in case lots (24 cans) with no mixing of brands permitted, but there's no maximum. In taverns, you can buy beer by the six-pack, but only two six-packs at a time. Of course, there is nothing to stop you from buying your limit of beer, putting it in your car, and then going back.

Trying to buy beer on Sunday can be discouraging, since about half the states prohibit or heavily restrict Sunday sales. In some parts of Ohio you can buy beer only on Sunday when you're eating at a restaurant. Other states sell only 3.2 percent beer on the sabbath. This usually means that you'll find only the major brands on Sunday as only they sell in large enough volume to warrant production of the weaker beer.

The percentage of alcohol in beer varies from state to state, but it's almost always less than the legal maximum. The alcoholic content of 6 percent beer, for instance, ranges from 3.4 to 4 percent. Ales tend to run one-half percent higher while malt liquor varies between 4.3 and 5.5 percent. Going down the scale, 3.2 beer contains .6 to 3.2 percent and near beer (such as Goetz, Schmidt Select, Kingsbury Brew, and Jet) has no more than one-half percent. Then there are non-alcoholic cereal beverages that taste like beer (such as Metbrew, Zing, El Sol, Dukesa, Disco and Steinbrau).

In the past, many states have placed tax labels on cans. Usually printed on the bottom of the can, they list the state, amount of tax, and percent of alcohol in the beer. These can be helpful in determining the age of a can. For instance, Ohio used a tax stamp from 1935 to 1964. Pennsylvania discontinued its stamp in the early 1960's, while North Carolina did so in 1969 and Puerto Rico did in 1971. The stamp disappeared from Virginia and South Carolina cans in 1972.

States still using a stamp include Alabama, Florida, Georgia, Mississippi, and West Virginia. At least one county, Garrett in Maryland, uses a stamp. Some Ohio and aluminum cans bear the stamp on top of the can instead of on the bottom.

Beer probably has come in more container sizes than any other canned goods. Over the past 20 years, U.S. brewers have used seven, eight, 10, 11, 12, 14, 15, 15½, 16, 24, 32, 64, and 128-ounce cans. The most common size is the 12-ounce can, which is available nationwide. After it comes the 16-ounce can, which is available in every state except Indiana and Ohio. In southeastern United States, the 14-ounce can is popular, and in the mid-south and Puerto Rico the 10-ounce can is widely sold. Once popular in western states, the 11- and 15-ounce cans are now being phased out. A few states sell beer in 7-ounce cans, while 8-ouncers are nationally popular as malt liquor containers. The 24-ounce can is produced only by Schlitz and sold in a few states, while the 128-ounce gallon model is only slightly more available than the cone top.

Canadian liquor laws deserve the collector's special attention because they vary sharply from U.S. laws (they also vary widely from province to province). In Ontario, for example, canned beer is sold only at Brewers' Retail stores—and only in 12-can packages. Although the packages completely conceal the cans, most stores have samples on display. Foreign beer, which sometimes comes in cans, is sold only in provincial liquor stores. In Quebec, you can buy beer in small grocery stores (not large supermarkets) by the six-pack or single can.

In Alberta, beer is sold in bottles only, while other provinces sell it in 11.5 and 128-ounce cans. Beer is sold only in provincial liquor stores in Alberta, New Brunswick, Nova Scotia, and Prince Edward Island, and it's not available on Sundays. In other provinces, it's sold seven days a week.

Stateside, there are also some unusual local laws and customs to remember. Some states charge more for a license to sell "high-power -ed" beer, so the collector may find 3.2 beer in some stores and "high-powered" beer in others. Some states tack on an additional premium for cold beer. In Pennsylvania, beer depots are closed on Sundays *and* Mondays. A few western states carry the word "stout" on malt liquor labels while some eastern states call it malt lager. In Indiana, the collector with children must take a babysitter, because you have to be 21 just to enter a liquor store. Indiana also permits no lighted or revolving beer signs in taverns. North Carolina forbids the sale of beer within 300 feet of a church. In the great state of Louisiana, laws vary widely, from almost all dry counties in the north to New Orleans, where bars are actually located in supermarkets. There you may sip on a mint julep while grocery shopping.

Beer's cost differs from state to state, according to state laws, taxes, lack of minimum prices, and promotional sales. It's probably most expensive in Alabama and Georgia, where it's taxed the heaviest, followed closely by North and South Carolina. In these states, counties may also add their own tax. States with the lowest taxes are Wyoming, Missouri, Maryland, New Jersey, Oregon, and California.

by Paul Ladefoged #39 et al

BEER CAN TRAVEL GUIDE

EXPLANATION OF TABLE:

This table shows the WHERE, WHEN, WHAT, HOW and WHO of can laws and beer purchasing in the U.S. as of this writing. Most information was obtained from questionnaires sent to BCCA members by Paul Ladefoged #39. The age minimum listed is the one for beer and may not be the same for liquor.

	WHERE							WHEN	WHAT			HOW										WHO
	Groc. stores	Tav-erns	Beer or party stores	Drug stores	Com-merc. liquor stores	Gov. liquor stores	Other	Days avail.	% of alcho.	Usual % of alcho.	Labels on cans	7	8	10	11	12	14	15	16	24	128	Min. age
Alas.	X	X						A	E				X		X	X			X			19
Ala.			X		X			B	E		H		X		X	X			X			21
Ark.	X	X	X	X	X			B	E	4-4½		X	X		X	X	X		X	X		21
Ariz.	X	X		X	X		S	BD	E			X	X		X	X		X	X			18
Calif.	X	X	X	X	X			A	E	3.6		X	X		X	X		X	X			21U
Colo.	X			X	X			AC	E		J	X			X	X		X	X			21
Conn.	X		X	X	X			B	E			X			X	X			X		X	18
D.C.	X	X			X			A	E	4			X			X	X		X		X	18
Del.					X1			B	E	4						X	X		X			20
Fla.	X	X	X	X	X			AT	E		I	X	X			X			X			21
Ga.	X	X	X		X		R	B	E		H		X			X	X		X	X		18
Haw.	X	X			X			A	E				X			X						18
Ida.	X	X	X	X	X	X		A	E	4.3-5			X		X	X			X			19
Ill.	X	X	X	X	X			BD	E	3.4-4			X		X	X			X	X		19
Ind.	X	X						B	E													21
Iowa	X	X					R	B	EG	3.2-4	HL	X	X		X	X						19
Kan.	X	X		X	X		R	B	FG		J				X			X				21U

	WHERE							WHEN	WHAT			HOW — SIZE IN OUNCES										WHO
	Groc. stores	Taverns	Beer or party stores	Drug stores	Commerc. liquor stores	Gov. liquor stores	Other	Days avail.	% of alcho.	Usual % of alcho. on cans	Labels on cans	7	8	10	11	12	14	15	16	24	128	Min. age
Ken.	X	X	X	X	X			BD	E							X			X			21
La.	X	X		X	X			BT	E				X	X		X	X		X	X		18
Me.	X		X			X		B	E			X	X			X	X		X			18
Mass.	X	X	X		X			B	E				X			X			X			18
Md.		X	X		X			AB	E			X	X			X			X			21
Mich.	X	X	X	X		X	R	BD	E	3.5		X	X			X			X			18
Minn.	X	X			X	X		AC	FG	4.4-6	JK		X			X	X		X		X	21
Miss.	X	X			X			B	E		H					X			X			21V
Mo.	X	X		X	X		S	AC	E	5	J	X	X	X		X			X	X	X	21
Mont.	X	X				X		BD	FG				X			X			X			19
Nebr.	X	X		X	X			A	E				X			X			X			20
Nev.	X	X	X	X	X			A	E	3.2-6		X	X			X	X		X			21
N.H.	X	X				X		BD	E			X	X			X			X			21
N.J.	X	X	X	X	X			AT	E			X	X			X	X		X	X	X	18
N.M.	X	X			X			B	E				X			X			X			21
N.Y.	X	X	X	X	X			BD	E	3.6-4			X		X	X			X		X	18
N.C.	X	X	X	X		X		AT	E	4.2-4.8		X	X			X		X	X		X	18
N.D.		X	X		X			B	E	5		X	X		X	X			X		X	21
Okla.	X	X			X			A	E			X	X			X		X	X		X	21W
Ohio	X	X	X	X	X	X		BCT	E	3.4-4		X				X	X		X	X	X	22U
Ore.	X	X				X		A	E	4-5		X	X		X	X			X		X	21
Pa.		X				X		AT	E			X	X		X	X			X			21
R.I.					X			B	E							X	X		X			18
S.C.	X	X	X	X	X		R	B	E	5-6		X	X			X		X	X			18
S.D.	X	X		X	X			AC	E	3.2-6	J	X	X			X		X	X			21
Tenn.	X	X	X		X			B	E							X			X			18
Tex.	X	X	X	X	X		R	BD	E	3.8-4		X				X			X	X		21

	WHERE							WHEN	WHAT	Usual % of alcho.	Labels on cans	HOW SIZE IN OUNCES										WHO
	Groc. stores	Tav-erns	Beer or Party stores	Drug stores	Comm. merc. liquor stores	Gov. liquor stores	Other	Days avail.	% of alcho.			7	8	10	11	12	14	15	16	24	128	Min. age
Utah	X	X		X		X		AB	F			X	X			X			X			21
Va.	X	X		X	X			A	E			X	X	X		X		X	X	X	X	21U
Vt.	X	X				X		A	E			X	X		X	X			X			18
Wash.	X	X	X			X		A	E	4		X	X		X	X		X	X			21
W. Va.	X	X	X			X		A	F		H											18
Wis.	X	X	X	X	X			A	E	4-5		X	X		X	X			X			18
Wyo.	X	X			X			A	E			X	X			X			X			18

KEY TO TABLE

A: Daily
B: Monday through Saturday
C: Sunday, 3.2% only
D: Sunday, after noon only
E: Greater than 3.2%
F: Less than 3.2%
G: Stronger in liquor stores
H: State name & tax stamp on can
I: State name only on can
J: 3.2% only on can
K: Strong beer only
L: Malt liquor only

M: 1935 to January 1, 1964
N: Discontinued early 1960s
O: Discontinued 1969
P: Discontinued 1971
Q: Discontinued 1972
R: Service stations
S: Discount stores
T: In most areas
U: 18 for 3.2%
V: 18 for 4.0%
W: 18 for 3.2%, females only

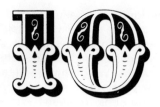

Canned Humor

As all beer can collectors know, everyone else thinks our hobby is, at best, a bit strange. So, fittingly, strange things often happen to us in our quest for the Holy Grail (Who brewed that, anyway?).

I remember one afternoon, sitting in my kitchen, sipping some of my favorite suds, when Jeff Berg (#799) burst through my door. After I had calmed him, he blurted out the story of "the lost treasure." Everyone has his moment. Ponce de Leon had his fountain of youth, Columbus had his new world, and beer can collectors dream of a mountain of cone tops in mint condition.

Once Jeff had passed the stage of being a candidate for the coronary care unit, he told me that he had just come from an antique store. After Jeff had told the owner that he was looking for antique beer cans, the owner said something like, "Gee, I wish I'd known that the other day. I was out in the country looking over an old trash dump and there were just hundreds of old beer cans around. You know, the kind with the funny pointy tops." Ah yes, funny pointy tops—otherwise known as cone tops—the rare ones.

Needless to say, the search was on. Jeff had gotten the directions to the dump, it was a warm day (we would regret that later), and we were both off in a flash. (You might remember the Flash was produced along with the Edsel, which should give you some hint as to how the rest of the hunt went.)

What the antique store owner described as glaring landmarks turned out to be something less dramatic. The directions hinged on a road that turned to the north and followed "a big irrigation canal." Actually, the road turned to the west and followed a small ditch. We all know about other people's directions. "Ersatz? Well, young fella, you can't get there from here."

Finally we were there, smack in the middle of an old dumping ground used by surrounding ranchers. Right off we could tell that there were some really old things in the dump: the discarded Spam cans, plastic plates, and aluminum beer cans told us that. There was some old stuff, it was a fairly large dump, and we were there, so we got out and started seeking our treasure. The first thing that hit us when we got out of the car was the smell. "Smell" doesn't adequately describe it—"stench" is better, but still not strong enough. Our noses puckered, our eyeballs bulged, and our chests hurt from trying to take tiny, shallow breaths. We both wanted that mountain of cone tops, but at what price? We both began to feel nauseous. What was causing that monumental stink. It wasn't Watergate; it was sheep. Yes, sheep, woolies, Montana blondes, Pendletons on the hoof, all quite dead. I'd say they'd been dead for about ten days.

Needless to say, we made a cursory examination of the dump and didn't see any beer cans of value, let alone cone tops, so we left in a huff. (The Huff was Nash's answer to the Corvette, which will give you some idea as to the success of future cone top hunting.)

Other strange things happen even on our days of mundane, ordinary can-swapping through the mail. I was very fortunate to trade cans with a nice gentleman in Sweden by the name of Gert Rasmusson. Gert and I had exchanged trading lists, picked out the cans we wanted from each other, and were in the process of overcoming the obstacles of our postal systems. I had taken great pains in packing Gert's cans because I know how our postal service treats packages. So, there I was at the window with my package of empty beer cans, thinking it was going to cost me an arm and a leg to send a bunch of cans to Sweden.

"May I help you, sir?"

"Yes, I'd like to send this package to Sweden."

"Sweden; you mean in Europe?"

"Unless they've moved it, yes."

"I think it's still in Europe, let me check. Yes, it's still there. You will have a few of these forms to fill out, let's see, two of these, this one in triplicate, a pink one of these, two of these yellow ones, and this card so we can notify your next of kin in case you have coronary arrest while you're filling out the forms."

Finally, after my writer's cramp had subsided I handed the forms back to the clerk.

"Well, let's see now. This one seems all right. Mnnnn, on this one you put down Gothis as your church preference. I don't think you understood the question. They want to know of what faith you are. Oh my, I don't think we had better put that down! Now then, articles in package are stated to be beer cans. Did you understand that question? They really are beer cans? It's against Federal Postal Regulations to send beer cans through the mail; I cannot accept these."

"Madam, that rule only applies to full beer cans; these are empty and therefore legal. I am a collector of beer cans and I am sending these to another collector in Sweden," I replied.

"I can hardly believe that anyone would send a package of empty beer cans clear to Sweden, and besides, I still don't think it's legal to send beer cans through the mail. I should check with the postmaster." Whereupon she dialed this mysterious functionary, hidden somewhere within the recesses of the building.

"Yes sir," she said, "there are nothing but empty beer cans in the package, but I thought I had better check with you. No, sir, he doesn't look like one. Yes, sir." Then, to me: "Here, he wants to talk to you."

"No, sir," said I, "I am not a hippy. No, sir, I don't have long hair. Yes, sir, I do have a full-time job. Yes, sir, they really are empty beer cans. No, sir, I am not sending any hippy deserters some of that Maryjuwanna. You can look in the package, but you'll have to be the one that re-wraps the package. I assure you that all there is in the package are empty beer cans. Just a moment. He wants to talk to you again." I handed the phone back to my Nemesis across the counter.

"Yes, sir, if you think it's OK. Well, he looks like a nice boy, but you never know. All right, thank you." And, at last, back to me:

"Now, then, young man, that will be four dollars and thirty-seven cents."

Small wonder that our postal system makes so much money; they're so efficient.

Another personal anecdote comes to mind, and that's my ill-fated trip to Yellowstone National Park. Living in Wyoming and not going to Yellowstone is like living at the top of Washington Monument and not looking across to the White House. So finally, after much coercion and procrastination, we left for the wilds of the Yellowstone country. The only thing really wild in Yellowstone is the traffic jam that starts at the gate and increases in severity as you near anything that's considered scenic.

Oh yes, there is one other thing that's wild and that's the "Great Campground Race," which starts every morning around six. The race consists of trying to beat 437,216 other campers to the 5,003 other camping spots that night. It's a great race, folks, and anything's fair except quad fifties and howitzers. Land mines are frowned upon but still used in some of the more populated areas of the park. Well, when we'd finally set up our camp, I couldn't hold myself back any longer; I had to have a go at the trash cans. Visitors from all over the United States and the rest of the world have been conned into coming to see the beauty of Yellowstone Park, and many of them bring their favorite brands of beer from home. Chances are, with that many people bringing beer from the four corners, you can enhance your trading stock greatly—and perhaps find one or two cans you don't have in your collection. Lust for the can was overwhelming, so off to the trash barrels I went, flashlight in one hand and pistol in the other. (I forgot to mention that Yellowstone has several muggings each season, and you can't be too careful when you might chance upon a rare beer can.)

The only way to search for a beer can in a trash can is to get right in there and dig. Best way is to spread your feet about 28¾" apart (this varies with the depth of the trash can), extend your arms straight above your head, tuck your chin in and, as gracefully as possible, kind of roll your upper torso into the can. If someone should happen onto you while doing this, I have found it best to tell them your wife accidentally threw her diamond ring away and you can't remember which trash can it's in. Ordinarily, they pitch right in, hoping they'll find it before you do, and in the process they throw out lots of beer cans.

As I approached the trash cans, I felt that old adrenalin coursing through the bloodstream. I hurried my pace and soon there I was at the first trash can. I extended my arms, dived in with gusto, and the cans started flying. I found Schlitz, Bud, Coors, and Hamms, all readily available brands, but I kept digging through that trash and then, my heart stopped. Could it be? Could I really have found a cone top here in the wilds of Yellowstone National Park? No, I couldn't have! I found a brake fluid can.

Not to be daunted by this grim twist of fate, I leaped to the next trash can and dived in. While I was mucking about in the depths of that can, I heard sounds coming from the next can, which resembled the sounds I was making. My first thought was that another collector was here poaching on my territory, so, without taking my head from the can I said, "What are you doing?"

"Gorf."

"What was that?"

"Growf; rumph."

Not being able to understand what was said, I pulled my head from the trash can and looked over at my fellow collector who had his head and shoulders buried in the next can. He looked out of the trash can and roared at me. Roared? My fellow collector was a bear, a rather angry bear.

I can't recount in exact detail what happened next. My memory is just a blur of crashing through trees, tripping over tent ropes, stepping on sleeping people, and bouncing off parked campers. I probably wouldn't have been injured quite as badly by the bear, but you don't stop to think about that when confronted by one.

It goes on and on. The curious stares as you dig through the roadside trash cans, the infuriated farmer asking, "You were looking for what in my barn?" We can collectors brave these little everyday inconveniences with smiles on our faces. We do expect some pity from fellow can collectors, but there are times when problems do arise, such as the time I had a Soul Malt Liquor can to trade.

Soul Malt Liquor is not the rarest can, but it is one of the most, if not *the* most, sought after among can collectors. Through a great

Dear, I think you're spending too much time with your beer cans.

deal of luck and much cajoling, a friend of mine found two of them in Los Angeles and sent them to me. The cans were in mint condition, never opened, and therefore almost priceless to a fellow collector. When I say priceless I should qualify that. Cans are never sold, only traded for other cans. Since I had two of these I had one that I could trade, so I placed an ad in the BCCA Want Ad list. Boy, was that a mistake.

As I said, these cans are highly sought after, but I didn't realize just how sought after. At that time there were about 2,500 members in our club, which means that I got just about that many letters. People offered all sorts of things for my Soul Malt Liquor, all sorts of other beer cans, naturally, but a litter of kittens, a used barn door, and three hub caps? As you might imagine, my mailman came to hate me. I think his last words were something about a hernia from the mail sacks. The mail was bad enough, but the phone calls! Calls from every place in the United States. Pleading voices, "I've got to have that can." Threatening voices, "If you won't trade me that can, I'll put out a contract on your dog." Telegrams, personal visits, endless queries. If I had only known the response I would get to that one little ad, I'd still have two Soul Malt Liquor cans.

Many moons ago, before trading in a monthly train ticket to the Chicago and Northwestern commuter line for a saddle, I lived in Illinois. As one of the then newer members of the BCCA, I was anxious to complete my set of Schmidt scenes. At the time, they weren't sold in every store you walked into, so we decided to make a weekend adventure out of looking for the cans.

I decided the adventure would include some neighbors, who weren't exactly fanatical about beer cans. But we packed up our genuine 1968 Plymouth Fury and set off to La Crosse, Wisconsin, in search of the elusive Schmidt cans. The drive went without event, and soon we were in La Crosse. We haunted a few liquor stores, without success. "!½#$!% □ $$$□ 9)$," I said. All the way up here, and not even one stupid Schmidt can. So, we decided to cross the border into the land of a million lakes, Minnesota.

Gold! The first store we went to had Schmidt's all over the place. After carefully sorting out the ones needed, plus a few extra, we passed through Wisconsin customs, and hit a few more La Crosse stores. Very little luck, but the mission was actually already complete.

. My completely bored neighbor (and by now, ex-friend) suggested we stop at the G. Heileman brewery and see if they might have a tour, and also something to quench our thirst. No dice, but they had a conveniently placed can recycling center across the street from the brewery. We parked the car and scrambled up the steps that led to the bin that was used. Peering into it, we found it to be quite an assortment of fairly common current cans. More Schmidt scenes,

Schmidt Select Near Beer, Ballantine's, Kingsbury Gallons, Potosi's, Hi Brau's. KINGSBURY GALLONS??!! Yes, before my eyes was a sight never before seen by a person from Palatine, Illinois. A whole herd of Kingsbury gallons. All out of reach at the bottom of the bin. The neighbor suggested we leave. The neighbor's wife suggested we leave. But they made a fatal mistake. They did not *insist* that we leave.

The faithful wife make a very intelligent statement.

"Dear, why don't you go inside?" I knew I had married her for some good reason. So, despite a few unheard protests from the now furious neighbor, in I went. The bin was about seven feet deep. I crushed Schmidt scenes beneath my feet. Coca-Cola cans writhed in pain. Fantas ran for their lives. Finally, I reached bottom.

"The police are gonna come, I just know the police are gonna come", hollered our neighbor. Let 'em, I thought, I'll can 'em to death. I reached for the first of the blue and white beauties. I tossed it up to my faithful wife, grinning like the Cheshire cat. She tossed it down to the not-so-scared neighbor's wife who packed them into the waiting getaway car.

"We're gonna be thrown in jail," he cried. I was trying to imagine why. Breaking and entering? Assault? Noise pollution? Finally, the mother lode ran dry. There were only a dozen. As I crawled out of the bin, I noticed Mike (the neighbor) peering out from behind a tree.

"Are you finished?" he gasped.

"Yes, Mike, we can make our escape now. I'll drive."

The caper was almost done. We got them home and washed them out, several times. The poor things smelled terrible. We stashed the loot until a future trade session when they became the cans of the hour.

I wonder if my trading partners at that session know that they traded for "hot cans"?

People think we're a bit strange, but they will go out of their way to help. Through a friend of a friend I contacted two women in England who sent me three boxes of English beer cans with the enclosed note: "Always knew you Yanks were a bit starkers, but glad we could help you out."

by Mike Davis #728 and Jeff Berg #799 et al

Happiness is...
A box
of beer cans

in your
mail box

Where have all
the breweries gone?

Americans today are drinking more and more beer, at relative bargain prices, but there are fewer and fewer breweries. Just before Prohibition, some 1,500 breweries were slaking the thirst of this country's beer drinkers. When the great experiment was over in 1933, fewer than 800 breweries resumed operations. By the time the beer can was introduced on January 24, 1935, only 730 brewers were still in business. In 1952, just 350 breweries remained. Some 210 survived until 1963, and by 1975 that number had dwindled to fewer than 70. Some industry experts predict only four breweries will be marketing their product by 1990. There will still be dozens and dozens of brands then, but they will be just like the Buick Apollo, Oldsmobile Omega and Pontiac Ventura are today—Chevy Novas, all produced by the same company, but with slightly different trim on each model.

Prohibition was the first peal in the death toll for American breweries. Many plants shut their doors permanently in 1920, although several remained open by producing malt beverages, other malt products, soft drinks, and ice. Many brewers that tried to open long idle plants in 1933 found their equipment encrusted with age. A few tried to use the same wooden aging casks they had used before Prohibition, only to discover too late that chemical processes, which hadn't taken a similar 13-year vacation, had made it impossible for the barrels to produce good-tasting beer. Other breweries couldn't find key employees. Many brewmasters went to Canada during Prohibition, never to return. This accounts partially for Canadian beer's reputation as a superior brew to its American cousin.

Smaller breweries also were hurt by stringent federal and state regulations which went into effect upon Repeal, governing packaging, alcoholic content, and processing. Some plants couldn't keep up and had to fold, even though they had good markets.

The beer can itself contributed to the fall of the small brewer, for it eventually meant that national breweries could produce beer on a mass scale hundreds of miles away from their intended markets and then ship it economically to those markets—and still charge less than local brewers. It is ironic that these large brewers, with their nationally-known brands, can price their so-called premium brands at a higher figure than a local label which often costs more to produce.

Many local and regional breweries tried to keep up with the national trend by increasing their brewing capacity. They spent millions of dollars doing this. Unfortunately, they sometimes didn't spend like amounts to produce a better product and improve marketing and distribution techniques. The Jackson Brewing Company of New Orleans closed in 1974 with a brewing capacity of 1,000,000 barrels annually. Falstaff, whose production for years has ranked in or near the top five American breweries, lost nearly $5 million in 1973.

Centralized food retailing has also contributed to the demise of the small brewer; grocery giants tend to concentrate on national brands or their own house labels. Local brands must depend on locally-owned retail outlets for distribution, but they're another vanishing American species.

And as our society becomes increasingly mobile, new arrivals in town find it comforting to see their favorite national brand from back home on sale in their new city, so they buy it instead of the strange local.

But television, perhaps more than anything else, has contributed to the dominance of a few national brands. Sold from New York to California, they're easily recognized by the consumer as he moves from region to region. And as Americans drink an increasing percentage of their beer at home, it's comforting to sit in front of the television set and hear how great those national brews are.

Local brewers have complained in recent years of unfair price cutting techniques by the national giants, but the large breweries have done this primarily to undermine the sales of other national powers. Major brewers, in fact, sometimes welcome strong local competition because it helps keep up the price of all national brands in an area.

The trend toward a few large breweries, though, is irreversible. And it is small comfort that this isn't just an American phenomenon. Great Britain 50 years ago boasted some 2,900 breweries. Today only 175 remain, and many of them are controlled by the six largest brewing companies there. Collectors may bemoan this worldwide trend and do all they can to support their local brewery, but their favorite will sink or swim regardless of all their best efforts. The ground was long ago prepared for the harvest now being reaped.

You'll find a list of all breweries qualified to operate in the United States when the beer can was introduced in 1935 in Appendix I. How many do you remember? How many do you think will still be in business in 1990?

As a further tribute to the small brewery, this chapter concludes with pictures and brief descriptions of several concerns which have fallen victim to the march of progress. As you read it, pop open a can of your national favorite and wonder what it was like when you had more of a choice.

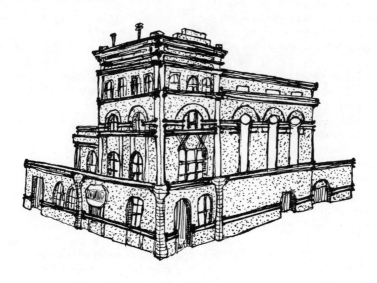

ANACONDA BREWING COMPANY
Anaconda, Montana

Closed in the 1950's, this brewery was home of Rocky Mountain Beer, a cone top. The building is presently home to a beer distributor and soda bottler.

TIVOLI BREWING COMPANY
Denver, Colorado

This plant still stands, although brewing operations ceased in 1969. It went out of business for the usual reasons—court fights, death of a strong president, labor disputes, a flood, and strong local competition. But Tivoli—a favorite hunting place for Denver collectors—stands out today for the special reason that it has been declared a national historical site and can't be torn down. Plans call for it to become part of the downtown Denver Aurora Higher Education complex, probably in the form of shops, offices and restaurants in the college area. This refurbishing hopefully will be accomplished by 1976.

The most desirable collector's items from Tivoli are the Top Hat and Heritage cans, although they're but two of the many brands produced by the Denver brewery.

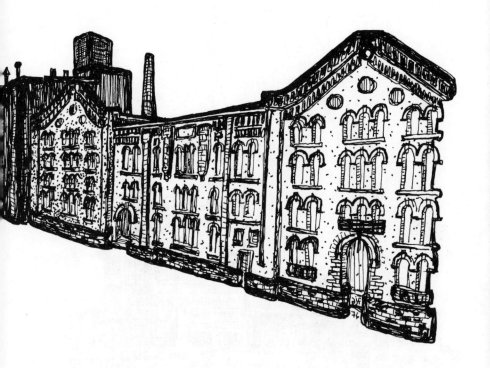

BURGER BREWING COMPANY
Cincinnati, Ohio

Burger closed in 1973 despite a million barrel capacity. Declining sales and labor difficulties put an end to the brewery, and it sold its brands to Cincinnati's Hudepohl Brewing Company. The real reason for Burger's demise, however, was its switch (in 1968) to artesian well water. The switch was made ostensibly to save money on the city water bill, which it didn't. The new water severely changed the beer's taste—and for the worse. As a result, many regular customers found something else to drink.

The brewery's most interesting can is the Burger Brau cone top. Also of interest is Burger Ale, which was available in later years throughout the south, but not in Cincinnati.

COLUMBIA BREWING COMPANY
Shenandoah, Pennsylvania

You are too late to see this brewery, because it was torn down in 1972. The brewery once had a plant in Columbia, Pennsylvania, but it didn't last as long as the Shenandoah operation, which closed its doors permanently in 1968.

Several of this brewery's brands are highly coveted by collectors, due to their limited distribution. They include Columbia, Whitman & Lord, Senator's Club, and Senator's Club Draft.

AMERICAN BREWING COMPANY
Baltimore, Maryland

This brewery closed in 1973, selling its American brand to the now-defunct Queen City Brewing Company of Cumberland, Maryland. One of many breweries to feature a statue of King Gambrinus, American also was among the first of many breweries to feature an eagle on its labels. Despite use of all the right symbols, American couldn't compete with local area plants of three large national or regional brewers and finally went under. Its architecture is unusually ornate for a brewery.

LITTLE SWITZERLAND BREWING COMPANY
Huntington, West Virginia

Proudly proclaiming itself to be West Virginia's largest brewery, the former Fesenmeier Brewing Company always forgot to mention it was the state's *only* brewery. When new owners took over from the Fesenmeier family in 1969, they tried to revive the West Virginia brand, as well as introduce two new brands—Charge in cans and bottles, and Innkeeper in bottles only. Despite an imaginative ad campaign for Charge ("Take Charge—the bold American beer"), their effort was short lived. The facility was soon sold to August Wagner, which planned to brew its Augustiner Beer there, but the plan failed when Wagner itself went out of business.

HAFFENREFFER BREWING COMPANY
Boston, Massachusetts

Haffenreffer closed in late 1964, selling its labels to Narragansett Brewing Company. After a brief experiment with the Haffenreffer Beer and Malt Liquor labels, though, Narragansett discontinued them—at least in cans. Haffenreffer's ale—called Pickwick Brew—was one of the most famous brands ever produced. Appearing in the late 1950 s, it billed itself as "the only blend of lager beer, light ale, and malt liquor ever canned in the United States." Not to be confused with the later Pickwick Brew Beer, the product claimed to be "an amazing beer discovery." Any collector can say the same when he finds one of the cans.

TENNESSEE BREWING Co.
Memphis, Tennessee

High on the bluff at Memphis, Tennessee, overlooking the Mississippi River, stands a monument to a once great Southern brewery. This large Victorian complex once housed the Tennessee Brewing Co., a leader in early brewery production.

Founded in 1885 by J.W. Schorr, Casper Koehler, and associates, it soon became one of the largest breweries of the era. The first beer marketed was named simply "Pilsener". Later, there were two brands called "Columbian" and "Erlanger"; this was, of course, before the period of cans. The best known and the leading beer sold in Memphis for many years was "Goldcrest", which after 1938 was known as "Goldcrest '51", to honor more than 51 years in the brewing business.

At one time, more than 1,500 workers owed their livelihood to the Tennessee Brewing Co., which is some indication of its size. By 1903, production was up to 250,000 barrels per year, making this the largest brewery in the South. The building that remains today was erected in 1890 and is basically unchanged, except it now houses a scrap metal dealer and is in poor repair.

The last president of the brewery, Mr. E. C. Krausnick, great-grandson of Casper Koehler, stated that even Goldcrest '51 was primarily a bottled beer and that they did not can ANY of their products until about 1947. The first can was a cone top, used until about 1950-51, at which time they added a flat top, produced until the brewery closed in 1954. Mr. Krausnick indicated that the percentage of their Goldcrest '51 in cans was very small. As a somewhat local beer, the brewery used the return bottles until it ceased operations.

CHRISTIAN HEURICH BREWING COMPANY
Washington, D.C.

The only brewery in the nation's capital after 1938, Heurich shut down in 1956. It is well known for its beautiful early Senate beer, ale, and bock labels. It also canned Christian Heurich Original Lager Beer. Its most famous product was Old Georgetown Beer, which featured a map of Washington with several historical highlights on its label. Among them, of course, was the brewery itself.

ENTERPRISE BREWING COMPANY (OLD COLONY)
Fall River, Massachusetts

This brewery's two major canned brands were Boh (Bohemian) Lager Beer and Old Tap Ale. It closed in 1963, passing its brands on to Haffenreffer and subsequently to Narragansett, which is now owned by Falstaff. Old Tap did not survive the closing, although Boh is still available. The Haffenreffer family was actually the active force behind this brewery, as they were with Narragansett.

JAX ICE AND COLD STORAGE COMPANY
Jacksonville, Florida

This brewery, a favorite of all Southern collectors, ceased operations in 1957. It was famous for Jax Beer, not to be confused with the New Orleans variety. Other hard-to-get brands it produced are Old Union and Sans Souci. Jax also is rumored to have canned its Peninsula Ale, although proof hasn't been found.

AZTEC BREWING COMPANY
San Diego, California

Opened in 1933, Aztec sold out to Altes of Detroit in 1948 and operated under that name until its closing in 1953. Its major brand was the Old Dutch cone top, one of two beers to feature a picture of "The Laughing Cavalier" (the other was Hals, a Maryland beer). When Altes purchased the plant, it discontinued Aztec brands in favor of its own. It also canned 7-11 beer while it owned the brewery.

DIAMOND SPRING BREWING COMPANY
Lawrence, Massachusetts

Owned and operated by the Holihan family, this brewery's major brand was Holihans Beer. Its most famous can was Holihan's Genuine Draft gallon. Produced in 1965, it was the only gallon can to come out of New England. Its most unusual can was Golden Brew, produced in the late 1950's. It was filled with lager, ale, or bock, with only the lid telling the customer what he was getting. The brewery closed in 1970, but the Holihan's brand is kept alive by the Hull Brewing Company of New Haven, Conn.

BURKE BREWERY, INCORPORATED
Long Island, New York

This small brewery reorganized in 1949 as Arthur Guinness and Son, Incorporated. Guinness continued to produce Burke Ale, but also tried an American version of its world famous stout. It imported special grains from Ireland, and the resulting brew tasted almost identical to the original. But the imported variety was still available and sales never reached expectations. As a result, the brewery closed in 1953. Guinness continued its experiment, however, with the Goebel Brewing Company in Michigan and California. Goebel canned both Guiness Lager and Ale, but the Burke Brewery never canned any product other than its own.

APPENDIX I

STATE-BY-STATE LIST OF BREWERIES QUALIFIED TO OPERATE AS OF JANUARY, 1935

52 = also operating in 1952   63 = also operating in 1963
74 = also operating in 1974
( ) = change of name as of year following.
Indented listing = not operating January 1935; but operating as of date listed following name, or earlier.

* still active

NAME OF BREWERY	LOCATION
ALASKA	
Fairbanks	Fairbanks
Pioneer	Fairbanks
ARIZONA	
* Arizona,51,63,(National)74	Phoenix
CALIFORNIA	
Acme,51,(Hamms)63,74-closed	Los Angeles
Acme,52	San Francisco
Ambassador	Los Angeles
American Sake	Los Angeles
* Anchor,52,(Steam)63,74	San Francisco
* Anheuser-Busch,63,74	Los Angeles
Aztec,(Altes)52	San Diego
Bailey	Rosemead
Balboa	Los Angeles
California Sake	San Francisco
Capitol	Sacramento
Cereal Products Refining Corp.	San Francisco
Louis Eckert	Los Angeles
El Dorado,52	Stockton
El Rey	San Francisco
Fresno	Fresno
*General,(Lucky Lager)52,63,	
(General)74	San Francisco
Globe	San Francisco
Golden West,(Goebel)52	Oakland
Grace Bros.,52,63	Santa Rosa
Grace Bros.-Southern Brg.52,63	Los Angeles
Humboldt Malt & Brg.	Eureka
K. Igarashi	Loomis
Imperial	Marvilla Park, Los Angeles
Koch	Los Angeles
*Los Angeles,52,(Pabst)63,74	Los Angeles
* Lucky Lager 52,63,(Miller)74	Azusa
Lynwood	Lynwood
*Maier,52,63,(General)74	Los Angeles
Aiji Matsuo	San Francisco

Milwaukee Bry. of San Francisco, (San Francisco)52, (Burgemeister)63, (Falstaff)74	San Francisco
Modesto	Modesto
Monterey (Home)	Los Angeles
North Star	San Francisco
Pacific, (Wielands)52,(Falstaff)63, 74-Closed	San Jose
Rainier,52,(Hamms)63,74	San Francisco
Regal Products,(Regal Amber)52, (Regal Pale)63	San Francisco
Salinas	Salinas
San Francisco Sake	San Francisco
San Jose Sake	Oakland
San Jose Sake	San Jose
St. Claire	San Jose
Jos. Schlitz 63,74	Van Nuys, Los Angeles
Sonoma Valley	Santa Rosa
Uhachiro Teshima	Los Angeles
Vernon	Vernon
West Coast	Los Angeles
Yosemite	Fresno

COLORADO

*Adolph Coors,52,63,74	Golden
Ph. Schneider,(Colorado)52	Trinidad
Telluride	Telluride
Tivoli-Union,52,(Tivoli)63	Denver
The Walter Brg. Co.52,63,74	Pueblo

CONNECTICUT

Aetna	Hartford
Bridgeport	Bridgeport
Burroughs	Bridgeport
Connecticut Valley	Meriden
Cremo,52	New Britain
Elm City	New Haven
*Hull,52,63,74	New Haven
Largay	Waterbury
Old England	Derby
Rex	New Haven
Waterbury	Waterbury
Wehle	West Haven
Weibel	New Haven

DELAWARE

Bavarian Luxberger	Wilmington
Diamond State 52	Wilmington

DISTRICT OF COLUMBIA

Abner Drury	Washington, D.C.
Chr. Heurich,52	Washington,D.C.

FLORIDA

American 52,(National)63,74	Miami

* Anheuser-Busch 63,74	Tampa
* Anheuser-Busch 74	Jacksonville
Atlantic 52	Orlando
De Soto	Tampa
Duncan 74	Auburndale
Flamingo	Miami
Hialeah	Hialeah
Interbrew,U.S.A.,Ltd.74	Hialeah
Jax Ice & Cold Storage,(Jax Brg Co)52	Jacksonville
* Jos. Schlitz 63,74	Tampa
Southern 52,(International)63	Tampa
Spearman 52,63	Pensacola
Sunshine	West Palm Beach
Tampa-Florida,52	Tampa
Wagner	Miami

GEORGIA

Atlanta Ice & Bottling Co.	Atlanta
Atlantic 52	Atlanta
Carling 63	Atlanta
Pabst 74	Pabst

HAWAII

American,52	Honolulu
Fuji Sake 52,63	Honolulu
Hawaii,52,63,(Div. Schlitz)74	Honolulu
Honolulu Sake Bry & Ice Co.,52,63	Honolulu
Kanda Shokai	Honolulu
Nichibei Shuzo Kabushiki Kaisha52	Hilo

IDAHO

Bohemian,52	Boise
East Idaho 52	Pocatello
Overland Beverage	Nampa
Sunset Mercantile Co.	Wallace

ILLINOIS

Acme	Joliet
Ambrosia 52	Chicago
Anheuser-Busch	Chicago
Atlantic,52,63	Chicago
Atlas,52	Chicago
Best,52,63	Chicago
Birk Brothers	Chicago
Bismarck	Chicago
Bluff City,52	Alton
Bohemian 52	Joliet
Canadian Ace 52,63	Chicago
Central	East St. Louis
Chicago Heights	Chicago Heights
Dick Bros.,52	Quincy
Fecker	Danville
Peter Fox	Chicago

Fritz	Freeport
Gipps,52	Peoria
Galena	Galena
Gambrinus	Chicago
Garden City	Chicago
Great Lakes	Calumet City
*Griesedieck Western,52, (Carling)63,74	Belleville
*Peter Hand,52,63,74	Chicago
Hillside	Joliet
Hoerber	Chicago
Huntley	Huntley
Joliet Citizens	Joliet
Kankakee Beverage	Kankakee
Keeley,52	Chicago
King Cole	Chicago Heights
Koller	Chicago
Lincoln	Cicero
Frank McDermott	Chicago
McHenry	McHenry
Manhattan	Chicago
C.A. Mitchell	Mokena
Monarch,52,(Van Merritt-Bohemian)63	Chicago
Mound City	New Athens
Peoria	Peoria
Peru Products	Peru
Pilsen,52,63	Chicago
E. Porter	Joliet
*Premier-Pabst,(Pabst) 52,63,74	Peoria Heights
Prima	Chicago
Reisch,52,63	Springfield
Rockford	Rockford
Rock Island	Rock Island
Roosevelt	Chicago
Ruff-Riedel	Quincy
Schoenhofen-Edelweiss,52,(Drewrys)63	Chicago
Schott	Highland
Sieben's,52,63	Chicago
South Side	Chicago
Springfield	Springfield
Star-Peerless,52	Belleville
Star Union,52,63	Peru
Stenson	Chicago
Superior	Chicago
Thornton	Thornton
Trenton	Trenton
United States,52	Chicago
Wagner	Granite City
Warsaw 52,63	Warsaw

White Eagle	Chicago
Zeman 52	Mundelein

INDIANA

*Berghoff,52,(Falstaff)63,74	Fort Wayne
Centlivre,52,(old Crown(63,74- Closed	Fort Wayne
F.W. Cook,52	Evansville
Drewrys,Ltd.,USA 52,63	South Bend
Hoff-Brau	Fort Wayne
Indiana	Indianapolis
Kamm & Schellinger	Mishawaka
Kiley	Marion
Lafayette	Lafayette
Muessel	South Bend
T.M. Norton	Anderson
K.G. Schmidt	Logansport
South Bend Beverage & Ice Assn.	South Bend
Southern Indiana Ice & Beverage	New Albany
*Sterling Brewers,52,63,(Heileman)74	Evansville
Terre Haute	Terre Haute
Zorn	Michigan City

IOWA

Blackhawk 52	Davenport
*Dubuque Star,52,63,(Pickett)74	Dubuque
Key City	Dubuque
Pointer	Clinton
Sioux City,52	Sioux City

KENTUCKY

Bavarian 52,(International)63	Covington
*Falls City,52,63,74	Louisville
Frank Fehr,52,63	Louisville
Heidelberg	Covington
Kentucky	Louisville
Oertel,52,63	Louisville
*Wiedemann,52,63,(Heileman)74	Newport

LOUISIANA

American,52	New Orleans
* Dixie 52,63,74	New Orleans
* Falstaff 52,63,74	New Orleans
Jackson,52,63,74-Closed	New Orleans
Merz	New Orleans
National	New Orleans
New Orleans	New Orleans
Standard	New Orleans
Union Products	New Orleans

MARYLAND

American,52,63	Baltimore
Baltimore	Baltimore
Brooklyn	Baltimore
* Carling 63,74	Baltimore
Cumberland 52,63	Cumberland

Free State	Baltimore
German,(Queen City)52,63,74	Cumberland
Globe	Baltimore
Gunther,52,(Hamms)63,(Schaefer)74	Baltimore
*National,52,63,74	Baltimore
Peoples Service Company	Frederick
Theodore Reichhart	Baltimore
Wiessner 52	Baltimore

MASSACHUSETTS

Boston Beer Co. 52	Boston
Bowler	Worcester
* Carling 63,74	Natick
Cold Spring	Lawrence
Commercial	Charleston
Commonwealth	Springfield
Croft,52	Boston
*Dawson's,52,63,(Forrest-Rheingold)74	New Bedford
Diamond Spring,52,63	Lawrence
Enterprise,52,63-closed	Fall River
Hacker 52	Lawrence
Haffenreffer,52,63	Boston
Hampden,52,(Hampden-Harvard, Div. Drewrys)63,(Piel Bros.)74	Willimansett
Harvard,52	Lowell
Smith Bros.	New Bedford
Star,52	Boston
Worcester 52	Worcester

MICHIGAN

A.A. Brewing Co.	Ann Arbor
American Beverage	Detroit
Auto City	Hamtramck
Bay City	Bay City
Bosch,52,63	Lake Linden(Houghton)
Cadillac	Detroit
C. & K.	Detroit
* Carling 63,74	Frankenmuth
Dailey	Flint
Delta	Escabana
Detroit	Detroit
E & B 52,63-closed(Merged with Pfeiffer)	Detroit
Eberle	Jackson
Flint Hill	Flint
Food City	Battle Creek
Four Flags	Niles
Frankenmuth,52	Frankenmuth
*Geyer Bros.	Frankenmuth
Goebel,52,63	Detroit
Goebel 52	Muskegon

Grand Valley	Ionia
A. Haas,52	Houghton(Hancock)
Haehnle(Hill Top)	Jackson
C. Kern	Port Huron
Kolb	Bay City
Manistee	Manistee
Marx	Wyandotte
Menominee-Marinette,52	Menominee
Mt. Clemens	Mt. Clemens
Mundus	Detroit
Muskegon	Muskegon
National	Saginaw
Old Holland	Detroit
Old Kent	Grand Rapids
Pfeiffer,52,(Associated)63	Detroit
Pfeiffer(Branch)52	Flint
Phoenix	Bay City
Pros't	Detroit
Schmidt,52	Detroit
Sebewaing,52,63	Sebewaing
Silver Foam	Battle Creek
*Stroh,52,63,74	Detroit
Tivoli,(Altes)52,(National)63,74-	
CLOSED	Detroit
Valley 52	Flint
Von	Detroit
Walker	Center Line
Wayne Products & Brewing	Detroit
Wolverine	Pontiac
Ypsilanti	Ypsilanti
Zynda	Detroit

MINNESOTA

Fred Beyrer,52	Chaska
Peter Bub,52,63	Winona
*Cold Spring,52,63,74	Cold Spring
Duluth Brewing & Malting,52,63	Duluth
Engesser	St. Peter
Falls 52	Fergus Falls
Fitger,52,63	Duluth
Ernst Fleckenstein,52,63	Fairbault
Gluek,52,63	Minneapolis
*Theodore Hamm,52,63,74	St. Paul
John Hauenstein,52,63	New Ulm
Kiewel,52	Little Falls
Mankato,(Cold	
Spring)52,(Mankato)63	Mankato
*Minneapolis,52,63,(Grain Belt)74	Minneapolis
Montgomery	Montgomery
Otto's	Mantorville
Peoples,52	Duluth
Premier	Fergus Falls

Red Wing,(Goodhue County)52	Red Wing
Remmler	Red Wing
St. Cloud	St. Cloud
*August Schell,52,63,74	New Ulm
*Jacob Schmidt,52,(Associated)63	
(Heileman)74	St. Paul
Schutz & Hilgers Jordan Brewery	Jordan
Yoerg,52	St. Paul

MISSOURI

A.B.C.	St. Louis
*Anheuser-Busch,52,63,74	St. Louis
Cape	Cape Girardeau
Capitol	Jefferson City
Carondelet	St. Louis
Columbia	St. Louis
Crescent	Marionville
*Falstaff,52,63,74	St. Louis
Fischbach,52,63	St. Charles
Gast	St. Louis
Griesedieck,52	St. Louis
*M.K. Goetz,52,(Pearl)63,74	St. Joseph
M.K. Goetz(Branch)52	Kansas City
Hyde Park,(Griesedieck-Western)52	St. Louis
Imperial	Kansas City
Louis Obert	St. Louis
McGovern(Appleton)	Old Appleton
George Muehlebach 52,(Jos.	
Schlitz)63,74	Kansas City
Peerless	Washington
Royal	St. Louis
Schorr-Kolkschneider	St. Louis

MONTANA

Anaconda,52	Anaconda
Billings,52	Billings
Butte,52,63	Butte
Gallatin	Bozeman
Great Falls,52,63	Great Falls
Kalispell,52	Kalispell
Kessler,52	Helena
Lewistwon	Lewistown
Missoula,52,63	Missoula

NEBRASKA

Columbus,52	Columbus
Fontenelle	Omaha
Jetter	Omaha
*Fred Krug,(Falstaff)52,63,74	Omaha
Metz 52,63	Omaha
Dr. Miller Company	Crete
Storz,52,63	Omaha

NEVADA

Carson	Carson City

Reno,52	Reno
NEW HAMPSHIRE	
Eldredge	Portsmouth
* Anheuser-Busch 74	Merrimack
NEW JERSEY	
* Anheuser-Busch 52,63,74	Newark
P. Ballantine & Sons,52,63	Newark
Bergen Brewers	Maywood
Burton Products	Paterson
Camden County Beverage Co.,52, 63-Closed	Camden
Columbia	Jersey City
Eastern,52,63,74	Hammonton
Egg Harbor	Egg Harbor City
Elizabeth	Elizabeth
Christian Feiganspan	Newark
Garden State	Belleville
Harrison(West Hudson)	Harrison
Joseph Hensler,52	Newark
Hoffman Beverage	Newark
Jersey	Keansburg
Gottfried Krueger	Newark
Liebmann 52,63(Rheingold)74	Orange
Old Fashion	Newark
* Pabst 52,63,74	Newark
Peoples(Metropolis)52,63(Champale)74	Trenton
William Peter	Union City
Schultz	Union City
Seeber(Rising Sun)	Elizabeth
United	Newark
NEW YORK	
American,52	Rochester
Amsterdam	Amsterdam
Peter Barmann	Kingston
Bartels	Syracuse
Magnus Beck,52	Buffalo
Ben Record	Watkins Glen
Beverwyck,(Schaefer)52,63	Albany
Fran D. Brady	Kingston
Burke(Later Guinness)	Long Island City
Canajoharie	Canajoharie
Canavan-Leggett	Niagara Falls
Cataract	Rochester
City	Ridgewood
Cold Springs Beverage	Auburn
Deerpark	Port Jervis
Dobler,52	Albany
Eagle	Utica
Eberhart	New York
Ebling	New York

Ebling	Brooklyn
George Ehret	New York
John Eichler	New York
Empire City	Brooklyn
Empire State	Olean
Fidelio	New York
Fitgerald Bros. Brewing Co.,52, 62-Closed	Troy
Flanagan-Nay	New York
Flower City	Olean
*Genesee,52,63,74	Rochester
Globe	Utica
Great Lakes	Buffalo
Greenway's,52	Syracuse
Haberle Congress,52,62-closed	Syracuse
Hedrick,52,63	Albany
Highland	Newburgh
Hittleman(Goldenrod)	Brooklyn
Huffel	New York
Hornell,52,63	Hornell
Horton Pilsener Brewing Co.	New York
India Wharf	Brooklyn
Interboro	Brooklyn
Iroquois,52,(International)63	Buffalo
Kings	Brooklyn
Kips Bay	New York
*Fred Koch,52,63,74	Dunkirk
Koenig	Auburn
John Kuhlmann	Ellenville
Kuhn's(Chautauqua)	Jamestown
Gerhard Lang	Buffalo
Laurer	Binghampton
*Liebmann,52,63,(Rheingold)74	Brooklyn
Linden	Lindenhurst, L.I.
Lion of New York City	New York
V. Loewer's Gambrinus Brewery	New York
Moore & Quinn,52-closed	Syracuse
F.J. Mumm	Lockport
Nectar	Elmira
North American Brewing	Brooklyn
Northern Brewing	Watertown
Old Dutch	Brooklyn
Oneida	Utica
Orange County	Middletown
The Penar Corporation	Yonkers
Phoenix,52	Buffalo
Piel Bros.,52,63	Brooklyn
Pilser(Allied)	New York
Quandt	Troy
Riverview Products	Niagara Falls
Rochester,52,(Standard	

Rochester)63	Rochester
Rome	Rome
Rubsam & Horrman,52	Stapleton, S.I.
Jacob Ruppert,52,63	New York
*F. & M. Schaefer,52,63,74	Brooklyn
Jos. Schlitz 52,63,74-closed	Brooklyn
Adolph H. Schmedtje	New York
Schreiber	Buffalo
William Simon,52,63	Buffalo
Standard,52	Rochester
Stanton	Troy
George F. Stein,52	Buffalo
Tonawanda	Tonawanda
John F. Trommer	Brooklyn
Utica,52,63-closed	Utica
*West End,52,63,74	Utica
George Zett	Syracuse

NORTH CAROLINA

Atlantic Company 52	Charlotte
* Jos Schlitz 74	Winston-Salem

NORTH DAKOTA

Dakota Brewing & Malting Co.63	Bismarck

OHIO

Akron	Akron
* Anheuser-Busch 74	Columbus
Belmont	Martins Ferry
*Brewing Corporation of America,52, (Carling)63,(C. Schmidt & Sons)74	Cleveland
Bruckmann	Cincinnati
Buckeye,52,63	Toledo
Burger,52,63	Cincinnati
Burkhardt,52,(Burger)63	Akron
Canton	Canton
Cleveland-Sandusky,52,63	Cleveland
Cleveland Home,52	Cleveland
Cleveland & Sandusky	Sandusky
Clyffside	Cincinnati
Consumers,52	Newark
Crokery City Ice & Products	East Liverpool
Dayton 52	Dayton
Delaton	Reading
Christian Diehl	Defiance
Dostal Products	Bucyrus
Eilert	Cleveland
Forest City	Cleveland
Foss-Schneider	Cincinnati
M. Frank & Sons	Mansfield
Franklin(Riverside),52	Columbus
Freimann's Beverage & Ice	Upper Sandusky
Hamilton	Hamilton

Hocking Valley 52-closed	Nelsonville
Hollenkamp Products	Dayton
*Hudepohl,52,63,74	Cincinnati
Koch Beverage & Ice	Wapakoneta
Koerber	Toledo
Krantz,52,(International)63	Findlay
Lange Products	Piqua
Leisy,52	Cleveland
Lancaster	Lancaster
Lubeck	Toledo
Matz 52	Bellaire
Miami Valley	Dayton
Milan	Milan
New Philadelphia	New Philadelphia
Old Capitol	Chillicothe
Old Munich	Cincinnati
Olt Brothers	Dayton
Pilsener,52,63-closed	Cleveland
Red Top,52	Cincinnati
Renner & Weber,52-closed	Mansfield
Renner Company	Youngstown
George J. Renner	Akron
Squibb Pattison	Cincinnati
Standard,52,(Schaefer of Ohio)63	Cleveland
Star Beverage(Wooden Shoe)52	Minster
*Schoenling,52,63,74	Cincinnati
Sunrise	Cleveland
Vienna	Cincinnati
August Wagner,52,63,74-closed	Columbus
Washington,52	Columbus

OKLAHOMA

Ahrens	Tulsa
* Progress,52,(Lone Star)63	Oklahoma City
Southwestern	Oklahoma City

OREGON

*Blitz-Weinhard,52,63,74	Portland
William Roesch Bottling Works	Pendleton
Rose City	Portland
Salem,(Sick's)52	Salem
Southern Oregon	Medford

PENNSYLVANIA

A.B. Company	Scranton
Ashland	Ashland
Barbey's,(Sunshine)52,63	Reading
Bartels,52,63	Edwardsville
Bentleyville	Bentleyville
Louis Bergdoll	Philadelphia
Thomas G. Berry	Chester
Beth-Uhl	Bethlehem
John F. Betz	Philadelphia
Boyertown,52	Boyertown

Brackenridge	Brackenridge
Bradford	Bradford
Brownsville	Brownsville
Bushkill Products	Easton
Cambria	Johnstown
Chester 52	Chester
City Ice & Beverage,(Altoona)52, 63,74-Closed	Altoona
Class & Nachod	Philadelphia
Club	Greensburg
Columbia	Shenandoah
Columbia	Columbia
Daenfer-Lieberman(Buffington)	Allentown
Danville	Danville
Deppen Manufacturing Co.	Reading
George Doehne	Harrisburg
DuBois,52,63	DuBois
Duquesne,52,63	Pittsburgh
Duquesne(First National)	Stowe Twp.
Duquesne(Chartiers Valley)	Carnegie
Eagle,52,63	Catasaqua
Elk	Kittanning
*Erie,52,63,74	Erie
Esslinger's,52,63	Philadelphia
Melvin G. Fahringer(Sunbury)	Sunbury
Fell	Simpson
Fernwood	Lansdowne
Fink	Harrisburg
Fisher	Reading
Flock	Williamsport
Fort Pitt,52	Sharpsburg
Fort Pitt 52	Jeannette
Frackville	Frackville
Franklin 52	Wilkes-Barre
Freeland	Freeland
Fuhrmann & Schmidt,52,63,74	Shamokin
Galeton	Galeton
General Braddock	Braddock
Goenner & Company,52	Johnstown
Robert H. Graupner	Harrisburg
Greensburg	Greensburg
Wm. Gretz,52,(Delaware Valley) 63-Closed	Philadelphia
Grunewald(Peerless)	Philadelphia
Haefner	Lancaster
Hazelwood Beverage	Pittsburgh
Heidelberg	Reading
Helbs Keystone Brewery	York
John Hohenadel(Falls),52	Philadelphia
Home	Shenandoah
Homestead Ice Co.,52	West Homestead

*Horlacher,52,63,74	Allentown
Jacob Hornung,52	Philadelphia
Howell & King	Pittston
Hyde Park	Hyde Park
Indiana	Indiana
Intercoast	Dunmore
*Jones,52,63,74	Smithton
Charles D. Kaier,52,63	Mahanoy City
Matthew Kelley	Pottsville
Keystone Manufacturing and Sales Co.	Millvale
Chas. W. Kloidt	Columbia
Kochs	Williamsport
Kuebler,52	Easton
Lackawanna Beer & Ale Corporation	Scranton
*Latrobe,52,63,74	Latrobe
Lebanon Valley,52	Lebanon Valley
Liebert & Obert	Philadelphia
*Lion, Inc.,52,63,74	Wilkes-Barre
Lockport	Lockport, Lock Haven
Moose	Roscoe County
* Mount Carbon,52,63,74	Mount Carbon (Pottsville)
John P. Muldowney	Mt. Carmel
Munich	Reading
Neustadtl	Stroudsburg
Louis F. Neuweiler's Sons,52,63	Allentown
Northampton	Northampton
Oil City	Oil City
Old Lancaster	Lancaster
*Old Reading,52,63,(Reading)74	Reading
*Henry F. Ortlieb,52,63,74	Philadelphia
Harry J. Overstock	Easton
Oswald	Altoona
Penn	Steelton
Penn-Indiana	Indiana
Penn State	Lancaster
Pennsylvania Central	Scranton
Philadelphia	Philadelphia
P. & H.	North Lebanon Township
Philipsburg	Philipsburg
Pilsener,52	Hazelton
*Pittsburgh,52,63,74	Pittsburgh
Pittsburgh	Uniontown
Pittston(Liberty)	Pittston
F.A. Poth's Sons	Philadelphia
Pure Springs	Fountain Springs
Quaker State	Philadelphia
Rahn	Tamaqua
Reinheit	Scranton
Rockwood	Rockwood
St. Marys Beverage	St. Marys

Sayre	Sayre
F. & M. Scheafer 74	Lehigh Valley
Schaffhauer(Vollmer)	Philadelphia
Adam Scheidt,52,(Valley Forge)	
(Schmidt's)63,(C. Schmidt	
& Sons)74	Norristown
*C. Schmidt & Sons, Inc.,52,63,74	Philadelphia
South Bethlehem	Bethlehem
South Fork	South Fork
Sprenger	Lancaster
Standard of Scranton	Scranton
Stag	Monogahela
Stegmaier,52,63,74	Wilkes-Barre
Sterling	East Mauch Chunk
*Straub,52,63,74	St. Marys
Tarr	Tarr
Trainer	Philadelphia
Tube City,52	McKeesport
Union	Newcastle
Victor	Jeannette
Viking(Edelstein)	Catasauqua Borough
Wacker 52	Lancaster
Washington	Washington
Wayne	Erie
Weisbroad & Hess	Philadelphia
Windber	Windber
Katharine Wentzle	Lykens
J. Widman	Bethlehem
John Jacob Wolf	Philadelphia
Wyoming	Wilkes-Barre
York	York
Yough	Connellsville
*D.G. Yuengling & Son, Inc. 52,63,74	Pottsville

RHODE ISLAND

Consumers	Hillsgrove
James Hanley Co. 52	Providence
Kent	West Warwick
*Narragansett,52,63,(Falstaff)74	Granston
Rhode Island	Pawtucket
Warwick	Warwick
Roger Williams	Providence

SOUTH DAKOTA

Dakota	Huron

TENNESSEE

Atlantic Ice & Coal Co. — Georgia	Chattanooga
Wm. Gerst	Nashville
* Jos. Schlitz 74	Memphis
Tennessee,52	Memphis

TEXAS

* Anheuser-Busch 74	Houston
Carling 63	Fort Worth

Dallas	Dallas
*Galveston-Houston,52,(Falstaff)63,74	Galveston
Gulf,52,63	Houston
* Lone Star 52,63,74	San Antonio
Harry Mitchell,52,(Falstaff)63	El Paso
* Miller 74	Fort Worth
Sabinas	San Antonio
San Antonio Brewing Association,52,	
* (Pearl)63,74	San Antonio
Schepps	Dallas
Jos. Schlitz 74	Longview
Southern	Houston
*Spoetzel,52,63,74	Shiner
Superior	Fort Worth

UTAH

Becker Products,52,63	Ogden
Fisher,52,(Lucky Lager)63	

VIRGINIA

* Anheuser-Busch 74	Williamsburg
Glascow 52	Norfolk
Home,52,63	Richmond
Jacob Ruppert 52,(Century)63,	
* (Champale)74	Norfolk
Sick's Rainier-Eastern Division 63	Norfolk
Southern Breweries	Norfolk
Virginia 53	Roanoke

WASHINGTON

Apex(Hemrich)	Seattle
Bohemian,52,(Atlantic)63-closed	Spokane
Century,(Sick's Century)52	Seattle
*Columbia,52,(Carling)63,74	Tacoma
Ellensburg	Ellensburg
Goetz	Spokane
Golden Age	Spokane
Horluch	Seattle
* Lucky Lager 52,63,(General)74	Vancouver
Kitsap	Port Orchard
Northwest Brewing Co.	Tacoma
The Northwest Brewing Co.	Walla Walla
*Olympia,52,63,74	Olympia
Peninsula	Port Townsend
Pilsener	Seattle
Pioneer,52	Aberdeen
Sick's Seattle Brewing & Malting	
* 52,63,(Rainier)74	Seattle
Sick's Spokane	Spokane
Silver Spring 52,63	Tacoma
Spokane Brewing & Malting	Spokane

Star	Vancouver
Yakima	Yakima

WEST VIRGINIA

American	Parkersburg
Fesenmeier,52,63	Huntington
Monongahela Valley	Fairmont
North Pole	Fairmont

WISCONSIN

Arcadia	Arcadia
Ashland	Ashland
Banner	Milwaukee
Adolph Bates Bechaud	Fond Du Lac
Berlin,52,63	Berlin
Blatz,52	Milwaukee
Bloomer Beverage	Bloomer
Boscobel	Boscobel
Bower City Beverage	Janesville
Burlington,52	Burlington
Calumet	Chilton
Capitol of Milwaukee	Milwaukee
Cassville	Cassville
Century	Milwaukee
Christmann	New Lisbon
Cream City	Milwaukee
Carl Ebner	Fort Atkinson
Dahlke	Westfield
Denmark	Denmark
Effinger,52,63	Baraboo
Electric City	Kaukauna
Eulberg,52	Portage
Farmers	Shawano
Fauerback,52,63	Madison
Fischbach	Milwaukee
Fountain,52,63	Fountain City
Fox Lake	Fox Lake
Fox-Head Waukesha Corp. 52,(Heileman)63	Waukesha
A. Gettleman,52,63	Milwaukee
Grafton	Grafton
Gutsch	Sheboygan
Hartig	Watertown
*G. Heileman,52,63,74	La Crosse
Hochgreve	Township of Allouez, Green Bay
* Joseph Huber 52,63,74	Monroe
Hutter	Hillsboro
Independent Milwaukee,52,63	Milwaukee
Harold C. Johnson 52	Lomira
William G. Jung, 52	Random Lake
Kewaunee	Kewaunee
Kingsbury,52,(Heileman)63	Manitowoc

Kingsbury,52,(Heileman)63,74-closed	Sheboygan
Knapstein,52	New London
George Kunz	La Crosse
The Kurth Company	Columbus
La Crosse Breweries, Inc.,52	La Crosse
Leidiger	Merrill
*Jacob Leinenkugel,52,63,74	Chippewa Falls
Marathon City,52,63	Marathon
Marshfield,52,63	Marshfield
Mathie-Rudie,52	Wausau
Mayville	Mayville
Medford	Medford
*Miller,52,63,74	Milwaukee
Milwaukee Germantown	Germantown
Milwaukee Shawano	Shawano
Mineral Spring,52,63	Mineral Point
Neosha	Neosha
Northern,52,63	Superior
Oconomowoc	Oconomowoc
Oconto,52,63	Oconto
Old Lager	Milwaukee
Oldport	Port Washington
Oshkosh,52,63	Oshkosh
Peoples,52,63	Oshkosh
Perplies 52	Jefferson
Plymouth	Plymouth
Potosi,52,63	Potosi
Premier-Pabst,(Pabst)52,63,74	Milwaukee
Princeton	Princeton
Rahr,52	Oshkosh
Rahr-Green Bay,52,63	Green Bay
Reedsburg,52-closed	Reedsburg
Rhinelander,52,63	Rhinelander
Rice Lake 52,63	Rice Lake
Ripon	Ripon
Riverview	Manitowoc
*Joseph Schlitz,52,63,74	Milwaukee
Schonbrunn	Sturgeon Bay
Joseph Schwartz	Hartford
Semrad-Pusch	Highland
Star	Lomira
*Stevens Point,52,63,74	Stevens Point
Storck,52	Slinger
Two Rivers Beverage,52,63	Two Rivers
George Walter,52,63	Appleton
*Walter Brewing,52,63,74	Eau Claire
Walter Brothers Brewing Co.,52	Manasha
Wausau,52	Wausau
G. Weber,52	Theresa
West Bend Lithia,52,63	West Bend

Weber Waukesha,52	Waukesha
Whitewater	Whitewater
Wisconsin	Kenosha
Louis Ziegler,52	Beaver Dam
WYOMING	
Becker Brewing & Malting	Evanston
Sheridan,52	Sheridan

by John Ahrens #9 and Ernie Oest #108 et al

DON'T KICK THE CAN

The Beer Can's Future

The future of the beer can is a little cloudy. If some people have their way, it'll be dead and buried when it is just over 40 years old.

The beer can is many things to many people today:

- To the beer drinker, it's an accepted convenience.
- To the brewing industry, it's the container for the major portion of their sales.
- To the environmentalist, it's the chief target in the fight against litter.

And, of course,

- To the beer can collector, it's an art form!

Beer drinkers did not immediately accept the beer can. Bottle manufacturers fought the can with all their might, developing lighter returnable bottles and the one-way glass "can" to compete with the newcomer. In 1963, cans accounted for only 37 percent of the packaged beer market, but in the next 10 years they really caught on, accounting for nearly 60 percent of packaged beer sales by 1973. The canning industry feels the real turning point for the beer can was World War II. G.I.s drank canned beer overseas, and by the time they returned home, they had accepted the can as a beer container.

The following chart shows how the can has grown as an accepted convenience since 1963, as compared to one-way and returnable bottles.

**THE BEER CAN'S SHARE
OF PACKAGED BEER SALES**

**PERCENT OF
PACKAGED BEER SALES**

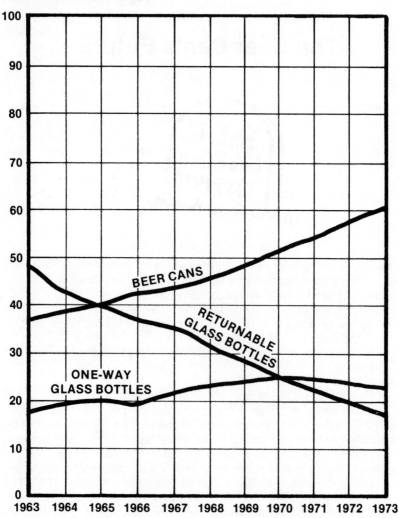

DATA SOURCE: UNITED STATES BREWERS ASSOCIATION, INC.

While packaged beer's share of total sales in the U.S. grew from 81.4 percent in 1963 to 86.9 percent in 1973, the can's share of the packaged beer market grew from 37 percent to 60 percent. Percentages can be misleading, so it might be simpler if we point out that canned beer sales jumped from 9.6 billion cans in 1963 to 23 billion cans in 1973.

While cans in the billions make collectors beam, they also provide one of the most visible forms of litter. Unfortunately, some people throw cans away rather than enshrine them in breathtaking collections. This causes litter, and "ban-the-can" has become one of the rallying cries for those wanting to do away with the beer can and other one-way beverage containers.

Legislation restricting one-way containers for beer and soft drinks has passed in Oregon, Vermont, and California; is being considered in Idaho; and has failed in Connecticut, Nebraska, Missouri, and Ohio. Environmentalists also have spurred the introduction of bills in the U.S. Congress, but at this time none has been voted out of committee. While the bills are sometimes tagged as "ban-the-can" legislation, most of them merely put a mandatory deposit on all one-way beer and soft drink containers, and outlaw the ring pull top. Of course, the deposit does reduce the number of cans sold, since consumers object to paying a hefty deposit on each can of beer. As for federal legislation, an editorial writer for the *St. Louis Globe-Democrat* put it this way:

Can Ban on Nonreturnables

The U.S. Commerce Department has responded sensibly to proposals for national legislation restricting the use of nonreturnable beverage containers. It has recommended against taking any such course of action.

As a department report pointed out, a federal mandate along these lines probably would do more harm than good. A study by Commerce found that the uncertainties involved in requiring a deposit on beverage containers seemed more likely to damage the economy than to help it.

The study was prepared in response to a Senate bill proposed by Oregon Republican Sen. Mark O. Hatfield and a companion measure which has been the subject of hearings in the House. Neither bill has received committee action to date.

Under the Hatfield plan, detachable openings on cans would be eliminated and a deposit required on all beverage containers. The proposed regulations would take effect within a year from date of enactment.

While it appears practical to encourage the use of returnable containers, as well as urging recycling procedures for throwaway cans and bottles, it could prove self-defeating to force consumers into a situation where they no longer could buy no-deposit, no-return containers. It could produce, in some, a reaction of no deposits because of no sales. The best way to handle the controversy is to can the ban.

Dec. 11, 1975, *St. Louis Globe Democrat*

The Oregon "bottle bill" has received a great deal of publicity, as it was the first such state law to be enacted. Since it passed in 1972, there has been a great deal of controversy over the effect it has had on litter. Two headlines used on articles about the Oregon legislation leave you wondering:

"Oregon Bill Reduces Litter"

"Oregon Litter Has Increased Since October Law"

As one can imagine, a considerable number of emotionally-charged arguments go into the passage of this type of legislation. Actually, though, the beer can is only the "tip of the iceberg."

Litter is a major problem, but when you analyze the make-up of roadside litter, some surprising facts emerge.

COMPOSITION OF ROADSIDE LITTER

Items	Percent of Total	
Paper	59.5	
Total Cans	16.3	
Beer and Soft Drink Cans		14.9
Total Glass	5.9	
Beer and Soft Drink (returnable)		2.0
Beer and Soft Drink (one-way)		2.8
Total Plastic	5.8	
Miscellaneous	12.5	
Total	100.0%	19.7%

Source: National Academy of Sciences-National Academy of Engineering Highway Research Board, "A National Study of Roadside Litter."

As the survey shows, less than 20 percent of roadside litter is beer or soft drink cans and bottles. The restrictions placed on one-way beverage containers, while well intentioned, result in severe economic disruptions both within the container industry and within the local community, and attack only a small part of the litter problem.

The economic consequences of adopting the Oregon experiment nationwide would be staggering to all beer and soft drink consumers. This tampering with the current beverage distribution system nationally would increase the price to consumers some $2.4 billion, which is far more than the amount currently spent in the U.S. for litter pick-up. This is a good example of what can happen when emotion displaces reason and logic.

Legislation similar to the Oregon bill was introduced in about 40 states, as well as numerous local communities. In some states the bills never got committee consideration. In states where they did get committee consideration, they were soundly defeated. In Dade County, Florida, one of the few places where a ban on one-way bottles and cans was put to the voters, it was overwhelmingly defeated.

Perhaps there is still hope. The brewing and container industries have initiated their own programs to fight litter and improve the environment. The best known is the "PITCH IN!" campaign by the United States Brewers Association. The idea behind "PITCH IN!" is to educate the American people to fight litter. The bumper stickers, litter bags, and TV commercials may or may not be effective, but they have been highly visible. "PITCH IN!" clubs are being promoted in schools and "PITCH IN!" weeks and months are being proclaimed in hundreds of communities across the country.

Coors "Cash-for-Cans" program, started in 1970, has proven an effective means to recycle aluminum cans. Coors pays 15 cents a pound (approximately 24 beer cans) for any aluminum cans turned in at their distributors' warehouses. The distributors receive a 2 cent per pound handling fee from Coors when they turn the cans in at the brewery. More than 95 million pounds of aluminum cans have been turned in during the first 54 months of the program. This equals 33 percent of the cans shipped by Coors. The recycling of aluminum requires only 5 percent of the energy used to make aluminum from bauxite ore, which makes the program even more significant.

Any solution to the litter problem must deal with the entire area of solid waste and resource recovery in a way that will not only protect and improve the environment, but also will bring about the most effective utilization of every available energy resource, including solid waste.

A program in St. Louis, Missouri, provides the ultimate in solid waste management. The St. Louis Solid Waste Demonstration Project is funded and operated by the U.S. Environmental Protection Agency, the City of St. Louis, Union Electric Company, and the American Iron and Steel Institute. The system, started in April, 1972, burns solid waste at a rate of 10 to 20 tons an hour in power plant boilers to produce electricity. The shredded solid waste is mixed with pulverized coal to make up the fuel used to generate electricity. The city's refuse is first sorted to remove all metals, glass, and other non-burnable materials, then these non-burnables are further processed to magnetically separate steel cans for remelting into molten pig iron. There are currently seven more of these "energy systems" operating or in the planning stage. The energy shortage is expected to give a boost to reclamation and solid waste processing nationwide. The state of Connecticut expects to meet 11 percent of its electricity needs in 1985 by burning garbage.

The American Iron and Steel Institute estimates the energy value of the household garbage collected in the United States each year is equal to more than 290 million barrels of low-sulfur fuel oil, or approximately two-thirds of our oil imports from the Arabian countries.

The future of the beer can may depend upon one thing: innovation. Changes must take place or the beer can as we know it today will soon go the way of the buggy whip and button-hook. One thing is certain: the ring pull top must be changed to some type of opening system which will quiet the environmentalists (can you imagine an environmentalist being quiet?) and please the beer drinker. The ring pull top with its throw-away tab has been a prime target of anti-litter legislation. If you have ever been barefoot and stepped on a pull tab in the sand on the beach, you can easily understand the need for an improved opening system.

Coors announced in 1971 at the second press conference in its 98-year history—so it must be significant—a new beer can top to eliminate the ring pull. The test cans, made in Coors' own can factory, have two indented discs that can be pushed inside the can top. This top was test marketed, but never adopted. A new anti-litter opening system is now being tested by Coors. The new design has only one opening similar in shape to the current pull tab, but larger and shaped like the bowl of a spoon. This is pushed in and against the side of the can. It will be interesting to see what type of opening will be adopted.

American Can has developed a top similar to Coors' two disc design, which it promotes as the "Button Down" beverage can. To quote part of the copy on their demonstration can:

New Packaging Convenience. Two easy push-ins of a single finger opens both holes. One hole for venting. One for pouring or drinking. There's no ring tab to throw away. It's a miracle of convenience packaging.

And miracles are just what the packaging industry needs to stay in business.

Falstaff tested a new slide-opening top on a smaller diameter, taller can (strangely enough the same dimensions as the Coors can) in the Dallas, Texas, market in 1974. Another new "easy opening" top was announced by Continental Can Company in an article in *The Brewers Digest,* December, 1974 issue. The can featuring the new top, called "Envir-O-Can", has a laminated foil strip with a ring opener that is non-detachable. This "stay with the can" feature is specifically designed to eliminate litter caused by the standard metal tabs. Continental Can makes its new top can from either steel or aluminum, and either material can be used with steel or aluminum-bodied cans. The fact that steel tops work on aluminum cans opens substantial new opportunities for recycling high-value aluminum cans from garbage by means of magnetic separation.

Continental officials also announced that they attach such importance to the need of making litter-free tops widely available that they are willing to license other can makers to manufacture the new top.

Cooperation between companies in the industry can help keep the beer can alive!

Our Canadian neighbors are concerned about the environment too. The new Club Beer can from Kiewel Pelissier Breweries, Ltd., of Winnipeg, Manitoba, uses the new American Can Company "Button Down " top.

Budweiser and Busch beers have test marketed "Button-Down " tops, so there's a growing chance this or a similar opener will soon top all cans in the U.S.

There are other innovations which are less evident, but just as important to the can's survival as a container for beer and soft drinks. Reynolds Metal Can Division of Reynolds Metal Company announced a new lightweight aluminum can in 1975; it uses 7 percent less aluminum than Reynolds' current cans. This means they can now make 24 can bodies from one pound of aluminum instead of 22.

American Can Company also has developed technology for ultra-lightweight, seamless two-piece metal beverage cans. Universal use of the new lightweight cans could save an estimated 400,000 tons of metal each year, in addition to bringing significant energy savings in production and transportation. These innovations are important, because inflation has hit the canning industry hard. Beer can prices went up nearly 25 percent in 1974. Metal cans, which were cheaper than returnable glass bottles at the end of 1973, are now more expensive. Thinner can bodies, which use less metal, can lessen the effect of inflation and help keep the beer can a part of the packaging system a lot longer. However, the brewing industry is committed to the use of cans.

A June 25, 1974, *Wall Street Journal* article announced that Schlitz is building three new can plants in Winston-Salem, North Carolina; Syracuse, New York; and Memphis, Tennessee, at a total cost of more than $100 million. Breweries making their own cans is not new; Schlitz already has two can-producing facilities which make about 25 percent of its total can requirements. By 1977, the brewer plans to produce over 50 percent of its own cans; Coors was the leader in producing cans; it currently produces more than 90 percent of the beer cans it fills. Anheuser-Busch has one can plant in St. Louis and another at its Jacksonville, Florida, brewery.

Miller Brewing Company plans to build a $20 million can manufacturing plant at its Fort Worth, Texas, brewery. When fully operational in 1976, the plant will produce over 475 million aluminum cans each year.

Coors' long-time can manufacturing commitment, together with

Anheuser-Busch, Schlitz, and Miller's investments, indicates that the brewing industry thinks the beer can does have a future. The editor of *Package Engineering,* in his March, 1974 editorial about Oregon's "bottle bill" placed this charge before his readers:

> The message for packaging is clear. Users and suppliers generally, and the big can companies particularly—those which the law hits where it hurts—have in their employ the best and brightest of packaging's talent. They now face a challenging mandate to innovate, to come up with new concepts. And instead of brewers, bottlers, and can makers diluting their efforts in a costly, delaying, rear-guard action, they ought to pool their skills, to create new packages free of environmentally detrimental features.

Thinking back over the announcements mentioned earlier about new opening methods and thinner wall cans, it appears that people in the industry agree with the editorial.

Innovation can also lead to new containers for beer. The Rigello container developed in Sweden is one example. The shape much resembles the cone top can used in the U.S. during the '40s and '50s. It's cylindrical in shape with a hemispherical bottom. Extra wall strength is supplied by an outer paper sleeve extending below the rounded bottom to form a base. The neck is cone shaped with a flange that matches the top of the lower cylinder; the two are assembled by "welding" the flanges together and crimping them over the upper edge of the paper sleeve. Pripp Breweries are testing this container in a three-year program. They have an exclusive on it with the developer, Rigello Pak AB of Lund, Sweden. The container is lighter than any can or glass bottle now in use and is competitively priced. Whether or not the Rigello container is introduced in other countries by other brewers is yet to be seen, but consumer acceptance in Sweden has been good. When introduced in 1971, it captured 8 percent of the market; its share increased to 23 percent in 1972. During the first six months of 1973, it accounted for 26 percent of the Propp and Three Towns market. Drinking beer out of a plastic bottle seems to appeal to the Swedish people, but it's uncertain how the U.S. market would accept it.

In 1975, two British beers were tested in plastic containers with metal pull-ring tops. The beers were Worthington E and Carling Black Label. Results of the test by Bass Charrington, the brewer, are not available at this time.

So, things are happening. Some argue the can's day are numbered; others see a bright future. What will happen?

Is there really a bright future for the beer can? Mr. Louis F. Heeb, Counsel, Environmental Controls in American Can Company's Corporate Environmental Affairs office, was kind enough to editorialize a bit on the can's future:

So, things are happening. Some argue the can's days are numbered; others see a bright future. What will happen?

"On the returnables vs. non-returnables (and cans) issue, I remain cautiously optimistic that the nation's elected officials will eventually use common sense and reason in rejecting restrictive beverage container legislation as an effective cure for environmental, energy, resource depletion or any other problems the no-growth activists dream up. In short, despite Oregon, Vermont, and a few counties and municipalities having already opted for the simplistic cure, I expect the beer can to be around for some time to come."

And, here are thoughts about the beer can's future from some of our nation's brewers:

"Some restrictions expected on local levels but no total restriction. Greater emphasis to be placed on solid waste recovery and recycling."

Joseph Cuziwski,
Manager, Packaging Development—Marketing
JOS. SCHLITZ BREWING COMPANY

"Much will depend on the successful development of solid waste disposal systems suitable for municipalities. If these can be developed, so that substantial amounts of metals and papers can be salvaged and recycled economically, the can has a long and healthy future. Since we believe strongly that re-use is the key to better use of our resources, our company has recently switched to aluminum cans, and will shortly be opening reclaiming centers. We are hopeful of recycling a substantial proportion of all cans sold. Other factors that will affect the can is the possibility of a biodegradable plastic container. Such a container, if non-breakable, lightweight, and economical could displace the can. We do not believe at this time that the can will be outlawed due to ecology."

F.X. Matt, II,
Vice President/Production
THE WEST END BREWING COMPANY

"They're here to stay. No, they will not be outlawed due to ecology."

Richard L. Yuengling,
President
D.G. YUENGLING & SON, INC.

"Current trend indicates that the cans will be around for a long time."

Joe Roller,
Office Manager
SPOETZL BREWERY, INC.

"No viable substitute presently in sight. Can may be partially restricted—"outlawed" is probably too strong a word."

Robert F. Agne,
Director, Market Planning & Research
STROH BREWERY COMPANY

"Assuming that the long range answer to solid waste disposal is salvage and recycle of the valuable components, the aluminum beverage container looms as the environmental packaging material of the future.

"There is no getting around the fact that if beer is to be packaged for home consumption, considerable quantities of solid waste or trash will be generated regardless of the type of package used.

"The aluminum can generates about one half the solid waste of the returnable bottles. But even more importantly, the salvage and recycle value of the solid waste pile from the use of aluminum cans is more than six times that of returnable bottles and steel cans.

"At 90 percent return rate — our goal for the Coors "cash-for-cans" recycling program (which offers 15 cents a pound for aluminum beverage cans regardless of brand at any Coors distributorship redemption center in our 11-state marketing area)—the aluminum can is superior to all other carbonated beverage containers as to litter and solid waste generation, cost to the consumer, consumer convenience, safety and energy consumption."

Lynn Weaver,
Asst. Dir., Public Relations
ADOLPH COORS COMPANY

'Growth will continue. Economic forces will outweigh ecology consideration."

Jack Genier
Market Planning Mgr.
THE GENESEE BREWING COMPANY

by Bob McClure #104 et al

GRIN AND BEAR IT

by George Lichty, Courtesy
of Field Newspaper Syndicate.

"The enviromental people after us, chief. . . . They want us to design a beer can that will look pretty as a wildflower beside the road!"

INDEX TO BEER CANS

INDEX